D0853930

THE RUSSIAN INTELLIGENTSIA

THE HARRIMAN LECTURES

Thanks to the generosity and foresight of the W. Averell Harriman family, the annual Harriman Lecture has become an important intellectual event and celebration in the academic calendar of the Institute and Columbia University. Previous Harriman Lectures have been delivered by the noted American social scientist Barrington Moore, the Russian academician and cultural historian Dmitri Likhachev, the late British economist Alec Nove, and the late British social theorist Ernest Gellner. In 1996 the lectures were increased from one to three, and a program of publication commenced with Columbia University Press.

THE RUSSIAN INTELLIGENTSIA

Andrei Sinyavsky

Translated by Lynn Visson

COLUMBIA UNIVERSITY PRESS

NEW YORK

Columbia University Press

Publishers Since 1893

New York   Chichester, West Sussex

Copyright © 1997 Columbia University Press

All rights reserved

Library of Congress Cataloging-in-Publication Data

Siniavskiĭ, A. (Andreĭ), 1925–

The Russian intelligentsia / Andrei Sinyavsky ;

translated by Lynn Visson.

p. cm. — (The Harriman lectures)

Includes bibliographical references and index.

ISBN 0–231–10726–9 (alk. paper)

1. Russia (Federation)—Social conditions—1991– .

2. Intellectuals—Russia (Federation). 3. Russia (Federation)—

Intellectual life—1991– . 4. Elite (Social sciences)—Russia

(Federation). 5. Russia (Federation)—Politics and government—

1991—Congresses. I. Title. II. Series: Annual W. Averell Harriman Lecture.

HN530.2.A8S56 1997

305.5'52'0947—dc21   96–53638

Casebound editions of Columbia University Press books are printed

on permanent and durable acid-free paper.

Printed in the United States of America

c 10 9 8 7 6 5 4 3 2 1

CONTENTS

FOREWORD

ANDREI DONATOVICH SINYAVSKY IS A MEMBER OF THAT remarkable line of intellectuals who have made significant contributions to our understanding of the human sciences generally, and of Russia and Eastern Europe specifically. His work and life are a testament to his commitment to freedom and opposition to tyranny and conformism.

Sinyavsky's life as a writer and intellectual is significant in relation to several important events. His arrest, together with Yuli Daniel, in 1965 and his trial in 1966 for anti-Soviet propaganda, were major milestones in the emergence of the human rights movement in the Soviet Union and a critical battle in the cultural wars of the Soviet intelligentsia. After he was expelled from the Soviet Union, he helped preserve the best of Russian culture abroad. The restoration of his Russian citizenship in 1990 was an essential benchmark in the reconciliation of post-

Soviet Russia to that part of its culture proscribed for so many decades since the Revolution. Most recently, his continuing powerful critique of current trends both inside Russia and in the émigré community demonstrate the vibrancy of that post-Soviet culture and the hopes we cherish for its continued flourishing.

Andrei Sinyavsky was born in Moscow on October 8, 1925, and served in the Soviet army during World War II. After the war he completed his undergraduate and graduate education at Moscow State University during the final decade of Stalin's rule. Sinyavsky taught Russian literature at the university until 1965 and was also appointed to the Soviet literature department of the Academy of Sciences' Gorky Institute of World Literature.

During the late 1950s and 1960s he had a promising career as a literary historian and theorist, but began in 1956 to write works he believed could not pass Soviet censorship. Because of these fears, he had them smuggled abroad for publication in the West. The first such work was *On Socialist Realism* (English translation, 1965; Russian original, *Chto takoe sotsialisticheskii realizm?*, 1959). That landmark essay was a penetrating critique of Soviet literary politics and practice. The first work to appear under his pseudonym, Abram Tertz, was *The Trial Begins* (tr. 1960; Russian original, *Sud idet*, 1960), a literary manifesto in which the author calls for the repudiation of socialist realism and for "a phantasmagoric art with hypotheses instead of a purpose and the grotesque in place of realistic descriptions of everyday life."

His scholarly and literary careers were brutally interrupted when he was arrested for alleged anti-Soviet writings in what became a celebrated case for the emergence of a small but courageous dissident tradition in the Soviet Union. The trial concluded with a sentence of seven years' hard labor. He was released from prison in 1971 and emigrated in 1973 with his wife, Maria Rozanova, and their son to France, where he taught Slavic Studies at the Sorbonne until his retirement in 1994.

In later works, such as *The Makepeace Experiment* (tr. 1965; *Liubimov*, 1964), *A Voice from the Chorus* (tr. 1976; *Golos iz khora*, 1973), *Little Jinx* (tr. 1992; *Kroshka Tsores*, 1980), and *Goodnight* (tr. 1989; *Spokoinoi nochi: Roman*, 1984), he sought to enact his literary manifesto of phantasmagoric art which harked back to the ornamental prose of the 1920s and the tradition of Nikolai Gogol. In *Soviet Civilization: A Cultural History* (1990), Sinyavsky provided a provocative and highly original survey of the major periods of Soviet history and its enduring myths and symbols. His most controversial book to date, *Strolls with Pushkin* (tr. 1993; *Progulki s Pushkinym*, 1975), mocks the official canonization of Pushkin in Soviet culture; it has earned Sinyavsky the enmity of Russian nationalist émigrés and native Russian nationalist intellectuals and political figures.

Throughout his life he has fought for the liberation of the writer from the political constraints of totalitarianism and for the liberation of the reader from the tyranny of authorship and the text. It is this voice of resistance and nonconformity that we celebrate in presenting this volume by arguably the greatest living voice of Russian literature, Andrei Sinyavsky.

> Mark von Hagen, Director
> The Harriman Institute
> Columbia University

TRANSLATOR'S NOTE

IN REGULAR TEXT, THE MORE FAMILIAR METHOD OF TRANS-
literating Russian has been used: for example, Yeltsin for El'tsin,
Moskovskaya for Moskovskaia, and Zyuganov for Ziuganov. To
assist readers wishing to look up references, in the foreword and
in the notes to this edition, titles and authors' names are spelled
according to the modified Library of Congress transliteration
system. When an author figures in both the text and the notes,
however, the more familiar spelling is used.—L.V.

THE RUSSIAN
INTELLIGENTSIA

CHAPTER ONE

The Intelligentsia and the People

I WAS RECENTLY INVITED TO PARTICIPATE IN A CONFERENCE in Italy on the problems of Russia today: perestroika, post-perestroika, democracy, totalitarianism, Gorbachev, Yeltsin, the Russian intelligentsia, and the roots of all this. When I began thinking about the past ten years, I suddenly realized that these had been the bitterest years of my life, for nothing is more bitter than unfulfilled hopes and lost illusions.

Before perestroika, I had a wonderful life. The Soviet regime seemed unshakable. It was possible to clash with it and to end up in prison, as had happened to me. It was possible to thumb one's nose at it behind its back, as many intellectuals did. It was possible to adapt to it—and even to love it. In a purely abstract sense, I understood that at some point it would collapse, perhaps in a hundred or two hundred years, but I did not think I would live to see that. There was no hope of that, nor could there have been any such hope. Instead, there was stability.

In the nineteenth century, the intelligentsia was very cautious in its attitude toward power. Traditionally, an intellectual who flattered the czar or groveled before him automatically ceased to be an intellectual. It is with good reason that Pushkin wrote "No, I am not a flatterer of the czar."[1] The intellectual's attitude must be very sensitive. He must not succumb to temptation, and he should not become part of power; rather, he should observe power from the outside.

There are many definitions of the intelligentsia. For example, a definition ascribed to the writer Boborykin states that an intellectual is a person who, first, has been expelled from university, and, second, who loves the people. But in the nineteenth century many people said that an *intelligent*, even if he was absolutely wrong in his thinking, was a critically thinking personality. Why do we say that the intelligentsia had a difficult time under Stalin? Not only because people were sent to prison and shot but also because the intelligentsia was disappearing as critically thinking individuals. If a person repeats all the obvious truisms of his leaders and his czars, how can you call him a critically thinking being?

Concepts regarding the Soviet intelligentsia were rather simple and clear. I, too, paid my dues to these concepts which, in short, stated that after the Revolution the intelligentsia was viciously attacked by the "victorious class," the Bolshevik Party, for its instability and inconsistency. An enormous list of sins was ascribed to it: individualism, humanism, flabbiness, excessive compromise, and failure to join the party. The major sin, of course, was freedom of thought, for while sympathizing with the Revolution, the intelligentsia wanted to think and reflect independently, not merely repeat the party's instructions.

An attempt to reeducate people's thinking lay behind all the vicious attacks on the intelligentsia. The "victorious class" had to free itself from that universal human morality, which it contemptuously labeled abstract humanism, and from any doubts regarding the infallibility of party policy. The spirit of intellectual, moral, and spiritual inquiry, those questions that live in each human soul—and not only in those of intellectuals—became a threat to the new society. This spirit was incarnated in the image of the unstable intellectual, whom Soviet literature attacked from the outset. In fact, Soviet literature attacked humanity and itself, as well as the remains of those intellectual elements that are an integral part of literary creative work. Soviet literature intimidated its readers—and itself—with the bogeyman of treachery. Show pity toward an enemy, and you're a traitor. Stand aside from the class struggle, and you're a traitor. Start championing the right not to join the party, or the independence of the individual, and you're a traitor.

The intelligentsia could not long resist such attacks. All interesting and useful work, all access to science, art, publishing, and education were in the hands of the state. The choice was either death or adapting to the demands of authority. Adaptation was chosen for the most sincere of reasons—a wish to serve the people. At the same time, this led to the decline of the Russian intelligentsia.

Ideas about the people were more complex and varied. One notion favored by some émigrés and dissidents postulated that since Russia was an occupied country whose people hated the Bolsheviks, once the Communist party was eliminated, the people would immediately become democratic. Another theory was that of the God-bearing people:[2] once the Communist party is destroyed the people will return to their Russian Orthodox roots. Others theorized that the whole problem was one of self-government, that every cook must be able to learn how to run the state,[3] but without the Communists. The overwhelming concern of the intellectuals who produced these ideas seemed to be the welfare of the people.

Suddenly perestroika appeared! Its beginning was so amazing that it was impossible not to believe in it. When the first perestroika issues of *Moskovskie novosti (Moscow News)* appeared in Paris, the émigré newspapers wrote that these were fake issues deliberately published for people in foreign countries in order to pull the wool over the eyes of the West. Soviet friends told us that the day *Moscow News* came out they would go to the newspaper kiosk at six in the morning to get a copy before the paper sold out.

Each day brought the intelligentsia a new piece of freedom: first free-thinking articles, then the publication of previously banned books, then Sakharov's return from exile, and even the release of political prisoners.

Gorbachev showered the intelligentsia with gifts, and at first it paid him back with gratitude. People joked that Gorbachev had simply read his fill of samizdat and was fulfilling the dream of Soviet dissidents by becoming the first dissident in his own Politburo. He was both the first Bolshevik reformer and the destroyer of the system.

I shall not deal here with the services that Gorbachev rendered mankind, for everyone is aware of them. He has already earned his gold or silver monument. Nor do I wish to discuss his mistakes, which were natural, since he was blazing a new trail. I am concerned with another question: why, after the August putsch of 1991 and the shift of power to Yeltsin's hands, did the intelligentsia abandon Gorbachev and go over to the new leader heart and soul? What was this—ordinary human ingratitude? The charm of power? Mass hypnosis?

The intelligentsia exulted, and the warnings of individual skeptics were drowned out by enthusiastic cries. For the first time in many years the intelligentsia had gotten a taste of power. The relationship between the intelligentsia and the authorities seemed to follow Mayakovsky's formula: "My militia is protecting me":[4] my power, our power, our union with Yeltsin.

When the first serious test of intellectual integrity and independence of thought came, that is, the implementation of the Gaidar market reforms,[5] which marked the start of a drastic split in the social stratification of the country and led to a situation in which more than 30 percent of the population now lives below the poverty level, the intelligentsia closed its eyes. This reminded

5

me of the beginning of the 1930s when the intelligentsia closed its eyes to the horrendous famines and disasters in the villages and maintained its silence.

I hold this against the intelligentsia and against myself. I had thought too much about the sufferings of the intelligentsia caused by official oppression and almost forgot how the intelligentsia had sold out. I realized that all of this had already happened in the past, that the intelligentsia had then believed that it held power, that it had in fact come close to the corridors of power, and that comrade Stalin himself had gone to have tea with the great writer Maxim Gorky.

The year was 1936. Arrests were in full swing. It looked as though the intelligentsia could get down to its major task of reflection and analysis. But that was not the case. Enthusiasm can be blinding. This is how the Russian intellectual Kornei Chukovsky described in his diary a meeting with Stalin:

Yesterday at the congress I was sitting in the sixth or seventh row. I turned around and saw Boris Pasternak. I went up to him and took him to the front rows. Suddenly Kaganovich, Voroshilov, Andreev, Zhdanov,[6] and Stalin entered. You should see what happened in the hall! And Stalin stood there, slightly tired, pensive, and majestic. You could feel how incredibly used he was to being in power, you could feel strength and at the same time there was something feminine, something gentle about him. I turned around. All of them had gentle, inspired, and laughing faces; those faces were in love. To see him, just to see him, made us all so happy. Each gesture of his was reverently watched. I had never thought I was capable of such feelings. Pasternak kept whispering to me enthusiastically about him. We went home together, intoxicated by our joy.

What strange words and feelings for an intellectual: to be intoxicated with joy on seeing power with your own eyes. Incidentally, a certain intellectual of my generation (who had learned foreign languages as a child and knew the works of Goethe, Rilke, Pasternak, and Tsvetaeva inside out) told us with delight that at a meeting with the intelligentsia Boris Nikolaevich [Yeltsin] himself had come up to him and clinked glasses with him. He didn't clink glasses with just anyone, the narrator hastened to add, in order to stress how exclusive he was. And this was a former dissident and camp inmate.

I have always loved old newspapers, really old ones. For the newspapers that deceived us during the Stalin, Khrushchev, and Brezhnev eras just a few years later were transformed into a unique source of information. An aging newspaper packs practically the same punch as cognac.

A few years ago, while working on an anthology of materials about 1937 compiled from old newspapers, we noted with sadness that all our writers had disgraced themselves. Literally every one. Irate articles and articles with artistic twists, by Olesha, Platonov, Zoshchenko, Iashvili, Babel, Tynianov,[7] and so forth, called for the destruction of the vermin, the enemies of the people. The letters signed collectively and published next to these articles also included Zoshchenko, Paustovsky, Antokolsky,[8] and Pasternak among the slew of signatories.

Listen to what they wrote. I have chosen names we hold dear, not those of the official bosses of literature.

Andrei Platonov: "Socialism and evil are incompatible. Today the cruelest form of evil is Trotskyism. This seeping virus of fascism tried to penetrate into the very heart of the Soviet people, to strike them dead at one blow."

Yuri Tynianov: "They are alien to the entire country, rejected by all who breathe its air, work on its land, sing its songs, and read its poetry."

Isaac Babel: "The language of the court transcripts is irrefutable and precise. The unparalleled righteousness of our government is more obvious now than ever, and our devotion to it is righteous and eternal."

Vladimir Lugovskoi:[9] "The bloody dogs of the policy of restoration came crawling on their bellies after their leader Trotsky, that trader in human blood and honor who has no homeland, that malicious degenerate and prostitute of fascism."

Samuil Marshak:[10] "They wanted to kill the helmsmen and take over the helm, to steer the country and all mankind toward a catastrophe such as has never been seen on this earth."

Nikolai Tikhonov:[11] "They had short slogans: Kill! Lie! Be vile! Sell out! Pretend!"

Viktor Shklovsky:[12] "These people are the incarnation of vileness. Their down payment to the fascists is the blood shed by workers injured in railroad accidents. They sell to the enemy the air our people breathe in the mines."

Note the style: "Look at them: puny, bald, wearing specs— henchmen of Trotsky." Or: "Slimy people who give you the creeps."

"This is stunning material, but very frightening," said Yefim Etkind, my partner in many émigré undertakings, as he was sorting through these newspaper clippings. A few minutes later, when he found a horrendous article written by an older man who had long been his friend, he added: "This stuff shouldn't be published." Nevertheless, we left in the material by his friend Fyodor Levin, who was a well-known literary critic, and writings by Marshak and Vsevolod Ivanov.[13] We spared only one intellectual; for we removed the Jewish poet Perets Markish and his gory verses from that collection. We felt sorry for his son, Simon Markish, a friend from university days who is now a professor at the University of Geneva.

With the victory of Yeltsin, the "democrat" from Sverdlovsk, history has repeated itself. Once again the flower of the Russian intelligentsia went over to the authorities, supporting Gaidar's looting and Yeltsin's firing on the White House, chanting: "Right on, Boria! Give it to them, Boria, go to it, Boria! Crush our enemies!" The marvelous Russian actress, Nonna Mordiukova, practically shed tears at one meeting with Yeltsin: "You're getting so tired, dear Boris Nikolaevich! Come see us and take a break."

No one thinks of what our children and grandchildren will say or whether they will be ashamed of us. Our times are interesting because they are so ironically congruent with our unhappy past.

9

But the final disagreement between me and the Russian intelligentsia was over the firing on the White House in Moscow in October 1993, which was supported by a great part of the intelligentsia—and by its most outstanding members. It was unbearably painful and shameful to see, at the bottom of those "collective letters," the signatures of cultural figures—Sergei Averintsev, Bella Akhmadulina, Bulat Okudzhava, Marietta Chudakova[14]—who on numerous occasions had written letters demanding that the adored president take harsh repressive measures against his political opponents and even indicated who should be sent to prison, which groups should be disbanded, which newspapers and TV programs should be banned.

What does the flower of our culture want from Yeltsin? What are these people writing to him?

The Communist and national-demagogic ringleaders are continuing openly and publicly to make threats on television. . . . They are counting on their ability to assert their impunity and their importance through bloodshed in the streets. They are hoping either to provoke a response showing the weakness of the administration (which has happened), or to produce "heroic" victims in their own right. They are looking for a Soviet Horst Wessel.

What should the president do?

All the political provocateurs who are trying to provoke rebels and hooligans, and who do not have immunity as deputies, such as Zyuganov, should be detained for their role in the May Day riots, and their organizations should be disbanded. The hooligan-deputies such as Anpilov and others should be deprived of their immunity.[15] If President Yeltsin and the executive and judicial authorities do not react harshly and quickly they will bear the political responsibility for the situation.

The president heeded this call and gave the intellectuals the tanks and the shelling of the White House. But the intelligentsia did not quiet down. Two days after the firing they wrote a new letter:

What is there to say? Enough talk. Time to learn to act. These dumb bastards respect only force. Isn't it time to show that force to our young, but—as we (to our surprise) have been joyfully convinced—rather strong democracy? This time we need to make clear demands of the government and the president to do what they should have done a long time ago, but didn't. All Communist and nationalist parties, fronts, and associations must be disbanded and banned by presidential decree. Publications such as *Den*, *Pravda*, *Sovetskaya Rossiya*, *Literaturnaya Rossiya*, and others must be closed pending judicial investigations. History once again has provided us with an opportunity to take a big step toward democracy and civilization. Let us not let this opportunity slip, as has so often happened in the past!

Appeals to the president from the intellectuals continued

throughout 1993, both before and after the firing on the White House. Among the names of people whom I cherish, there suddenly appeared one that was nearly sacred, that of Academician Likhachev.[16] But those shots were fired at the people . . .

This became a sticking point in my disagreements with some dear friends. One of my opponents' arguments was that if Yeltsin had not fired on the White House the Communists and fascists would have come to power, and a civil war would have broken out in Russia.

A group of my friends gathered at the house of an *Izvestia* journalist to prove to me, whom they saw as an old man abroad who was not keeping abreast of Russian reality, that their view was right. They showed me videocassettes of the crowds surrounding the White House, the people carrying red flags at the May Day demonstrations, and some other crowds. A very close friend of ours, a poet, teacher, wife of a priest, a sweet, kind, and religious woman lamented: "Just look at those horrible faces!" It was written on her face that shooting those horrible faces would be no sin. Those excited and aging people could hardly be described as beautiful.

I somehow managed to find the words to describe what was going on: Here I was, a guest of the contemporary intelligentsia, and the *people* were on the television screen. I started to understand that the intelligentsia, which in the past had lived with the people and shared its misfortunes to such an extent that the very term *intellectual*, which arose in the nineteenth century, unequivocally implied a love for the people, was today afraid of those same people.

Why? Why in the past did the intelligentsia pity the people, sympathize with them, declare "I dedicated my lyre to the people,"[17] but now tremble? What happened?

We have heard over and over that one reason for such panic is the fear of pogroms produced by the primordial anti-Semitism of the Russian people. It's true that popular disaffection was sometimes expressed in anti-Semitic movements. From my point of view, Russian anti-Semitism represents a kind of alienation of evil. It is a popular, mythic, almost fairy-tale notion that the people cannot be bad. Our people are good. They are *our* people. But some outsiders have wormed their way into the government, and they are to blame for everything. In the past I often had to argue about this with men in the camps, and pointed to the fact that the government, the KGB, and the courts were almost entirely made up of Russians. The major argument of my uneducated opponents was, Is a Russian capable of such injustice? These are clearly the ploys of outsiders or foreigners, because at heart we are all kind and good.

Yet I, who have fought anti-Semitism throughout my entire life, felt strangely reassured. And it was Zhirinovsky who reassured me. If such a large percentage of the Russian people could vote for him (and we should not forget that in 1993 he got some 23 percent of the vote), for a man who looks so obviously Jewish, that means that my great people is not so terribly anti-Semitic.

Today this myth has changed. Anti-Americanism has grown. This has been caused by the glaring abundance of foreign goods, which only rich people can afford, and by the fact that Moscow is now blanketed by foreign advertising, signs, and names that irritate me, even though I have been living in France for a long time and have no negative feelings whatever toward America. But it is irritating that Moscow sports an enormous neon sign advertising The Very Best American Tobacco, that this tobacco is unaffordable, and that your income is barely enough for a lousy domestic Belomor. It looks like foreign occupation. Cities are studded with signs such as Casino or Casanova Night Club (Great Intimate Atmosphere); a restaurant called At the Banker's; The Lolita Venereal Disease Clinic; The Flamingo Bar; and the Gallant grocery store. Just try to imagine such signs not in Moscow—which has anything and everything—but in the small, ancient town of Pereslavl-Zalessky, which has the Eden dry cleaners, but no sidewalks. Against the background of dirt and poverty foreign words sound like a nasty parody of Western lifestyles.

I think that today there is excessive freedom of language. There are all kinds of filthy language, as well as an incredible corruption of the language with foreign words. I have difficulty fully understanding some things that are direct borrowings from English. That also irritates the people. They don't understand what a *spiker* [a parliamentary speaker] is. They don't understand all those new words. They really hate that, and then they again think that America is the reason for all our misfortunes. I remember that back in the Stalin years, America was blamed for everything. So there are reasons for concern about what is happening to the language.

Russian shops and kiosks are inundated with foreign goods, and this parody of capitalism looks extremely vulgar and brazen. That capitalism, which is bringing a great many problems in its wake, is also associated with America. Moscow has become an alien city to Muscovites. Many houses on the main streets have been bought or rented by foreigners, and the local population has been evicted to the outskirts. The dollar is the most common currency and a symbol of wealth. A dollarization of consciousness is taking place, and is encountering a logical—and negative—popular reaction. Slogans such as Down with the Bourgeois! or Death to the Bourgeois! are more and more often scrawled on walls. These words fall on fertile Russian revolutionary soil. It was not hard to guess that the Communists would win the Duma elections.

In October 1995 we went to a large Communist meeting in Moscow. All two thousand tickets had been sold (and tickets cost ten thousand rubles, which is no small price). I talked to a middle-aged engineer. His father had died at the front during the war, but his mother, an ordinary worker who was left with two children, had managed to give them a higher education. And now, under the democrats, is he going to be able to educate his sons? Though he is not a Communist, he naturally sympathizes with them.

In December 1995 the Communists won the Duma elections. How does Boris Zolotukhin, a deputy who is a democrat, a well-known dissident and champion of human rights, react to that, and how does he explain the defeat of democracy? "The democrats were unable to explain to the people why the Gaidar reforms did not result in a real improvement in the lives of most people."

No matter how much you explain to the people why they are badly off, poverty will not be any more pleasant. It is understandable that people are asking the democrats, i.e., the intellectuals Yegor Gaidar and Boris Zolotukhin,[18] Why did you allow the people to reach this state of poverty? They answered their own question by voting for the Communists.

Zolotukhin also shifts the blame from the intelligentsia to the people:

> It is characteristic of Russia that the majority of people were reconciled to the fact that the guaranteed salary was wretched and that guaranteed medicine was awful. People who are not used to living in conditions of freedom are now feeling nostalgic for what they have lost. These middle-aged people cannot adapt to the new conditions. Even those who are ready to exist on a miserable salary and to stand on lines are not ready for an independent life and are not ready to stand up for themselves. They backed the Communist party.

In other words: the people are bad, the people are to blame for everything. And is half-baked Minister Gaidar in fact good? And it does not occur to Zolotukhin, as a jurist and a lawyer, that you cannot first rob a man, reduce him to tatters, and then turn him out naked on the street, telling him: "Now go survive on your own."

I recall with longing the far-off past, before the Revolution, when the Russian intelligentsia occupied the rather broad space separating the people from the authorities: when it was critical of the authorities and could not be otherwise; when a natural component of the intelligentsia was the so-called critically think-ing personality, as the intellectuals were called in the nineteenth century; when it was considered monstrous for an intellectual to grovel before the authorities ("I'm glad to serve, but fawning makes me sick," said Chatsky, one of the first Russian intellectu-als);[19] when the intelligentsia empathized with the people and felt guilty because of its relatively privileged place in society.

The intellectual of today seems to be saying that the people are nostalgic for slavery and poverty. In fact, the people are nostalgic for the past, when they lived better than they do now.

The meaning of life has also been lost, and this has had a somber impact on Russian consciousness. What did Soviet power give the man on the street? Freedom, land, and wealth? Nothing of the sort. All it gave was a sense of righteousness and an aware-ness that we lived in a properly run and logical world. We have now fallen from that logical Soviet cosmos into chaos and have no idea what we can believe in. The meaning of the lives of several generations has been lost. It looks as though they lived and suf-fered in vain. After all, it is hard to believe in the dawn of capi-talism, particularly such a wild and terrible capitalism, which smacks of criminal lawlessness.

Humanity often asks questions about the meaning of life and the purpose of existence, and Russians are perhaps particularly inclined to do so. In 1904 Nikolai Berdyaev[20] wrote that "the Russian yearning for the meaning of life is the major theme of our literature, and this is the real point of our intelligentsia's existence."

This is not only the distinguishing feature of the intelligentsia: it is also the treasured core of individual Russians and of the Russian people described in our literature throughout the nineteenth century. All of a sudden the interests of the intelligentsia and the people seem to have gone their separate ways, and they have stopped understanding each other.

Six months before the Duma elections of May 1995, the newspaper *Obshchaya gazeta* published a very interesting dialogue between the newspaper's editor, Yegor Yakovlev, and the Russian ambassador to Paris, Academician Yuri Ryzhov. Yakovlev speaks of the catastrophic situation in the country: "The Parliament has been disbanded, the President is endowed by the new constitution with unlimited power, feedback between the authorities and society has been cut off once and for all." Ryzhov consoles him. The editor is 10 percent hopeful and 90 percent despairing. For the ambassador, since he is an official and a bureaucrat, the ratio is 50-50, and that is why he is optimistic. Yakovlev is on the brink of despair: "The entire *Weltanschauung* of the Russian people today is reduced to the question of how to make do and survive." The ambassador does not object but merely makes a small correction: "You're right in saying that the masses are trying to survive. But survival is not a new ideology and not a new mythology. It is a natural, and to a great extent physiological, reaction.

Things will be easier for the next generation." "Nevertheless, answer me," Yakovlev replied. "If in April 1985 you'd told people what awaited them in April 1995, and called on them to follow you, would they have supported you? If you'd told them that they would be afraid to go out of the house in the evening?" "You don't remember how afraid they were in the past?" Ryzhov asked in reply. "Not afraid of going out of the house, but of the footsteps outside the door! They'd say to me that it's better to be scared to go out in the street than to be constantly waiting for them to come and get us."

Here Ryzhov is distorting the situation. Yegor Yakovlev is asking him about the beginning of perestroika, about 1985, when no one was afraid of steps outside the door because the time of unjustified repressions was long gone. The dissidents had never stayed up listening for the sound of steps at night, for they understood what they were getting into. Ryzhov, however, was speaking of the time of Stalinist repressions.

Even then, people were not terribly afraid of steps outside the door. For the most part, it was either the educated strata of society or the party bosses who were afraid. The people were sometimes happy when the bosses were sent to jail. In the camp, one clever man tried to prove to me that under Stalin things were better, because then the bosses were afraid to repress the people and their behavior was more restrained. He thought that all the bosses should be shot every ten years, the same way wolves in the forest are periodically shot to keep their numbers down.

Vassily Aksyonov,[21] whose father and mother were former

party bosses who rotted in the camps for many years, was indignant over the results of the most recent Duma elections. In the newspaper *Moskovskie novosti* he wrote:

> The people have voted. What can you do about that? What is striking is the cynicism of these "people" who have voted. So it turns out that all the unmasking of Communist crimes during the years of glasnost and freedom, all of those countless bullets to the backs of heads, were things about which they didn't give a damn?

Aksyonov puts the word *people* in contemptuous quotation marks. Academician Ryzhov is also displeased with the masses (that is, with the people). When the prior elections to the Duma did not agree with what he had predicted, Yuri Kariakin, a specialist on Dostoevsky (that is, on the people), exclaimed in utter despair, "Russia! You've lost your mind!"

The words Konstantin Balmont[22] addressed to himself after the October Revolution, when the people supported the Bolsheviks, are relevant here:

> You were wrong about everything: your beloved people
> Are not the people you dreamed they were.

The recent elections to the Duma were best summarized by the economist Nikolai Shmelev:

> The elections have clearly demonstrated that the Russian

population refuses to think of itself as mute cattle. Thank God it expressed its conviction through the ballot box, and not with grenades and automatic rifles.

Obshchaya gazeta, January 25, 1996

All that remains for me is to make a futile appeal to the intelligentsia by citing the verses of Aleksandr Blok,[23] written eighty years ago:

Open your eyes, and open them faster
to the unfathomable horror of life,
before everything in your motherland
is swept away by a great thunderstorm.

On October 3, 1994, the anniversary of Black October, my wife and I went to the stadium at Krasnaya Presnya in Moscow. A brass band was playing funeral marches. Some people were demonstrating; others had brought flowers. The Black Hundreds, who always know who is to blame, were bawling away. An imposing old lady stared blankly at me and said: "Well, I wasn't expecting to see you here. I thought the intelligentsia had completely lost its conscience."

I think that the intelligentsia was divided. Many members of the intelligentsia welcomed the firing on the White House. I think that intellectuals who were better off—not necessarily rich, but who were confident of their situation—welcomed it. The poorer intelligentsia, the teachers and ordinary people, naturally took the side of the people. The old woman who spoke to me looked like an intellectual, and she'd come to the memorial meeting on that sad anniversary of the firing on the White House.

Then we went to a demonstration at the Moscow Soviet where that lovely girl Novodvorskaya proposed that everybody drink champagne to the health of Boris Nikolaevich, little Yegor Gaidar, and the glorious tank crews that had done such a beautiful job of firing on the White House.

Today the intelligentsia is starting to see the light. While the intelligentsia did not cause a lot of trouble over the firing on the White House, in the war with Chechnya, thank God, Yeltsin has not gotten support. The intelligentsia's opposition to Yeltsin has broadened. I am glad that Sergei Kovalev[24] has returned to the dissident movement, and I hope he will feel more comfortable in this role than in Yeltsin's service. Every cloud has a silver lining. Otherwise our Sergei Adamovich would be serving as a human rights adviser to Mr. Cannibal. The intelligentsia, however, has not yet understood that the war in Chechnya is a direct continuation of the firing on the White House. Until my favorite group in society understands its guilt, good will not triumph.

I keep returning to the subject of the firing on the White House. After all, what's the Supreme Soviet to me? Do I think that Rutskoi and Khasbulatov[25] are such bright people? I really don't care about them. The Supreme Soviet is bad and the Parliament is lousy. But just because your Parliament isn't good enough is no reason to fire cannons at it. Can you imagine the

American president firing cannons at Congress just because some people are arguing with him? That's what I find so painful. Russia has had enough cannon fire. I'm against cannon fire in general. There's been enough use of force in freeing the country from czarism. When democracy sheds blood as its first step—I say that cannot be done. No. Period.

CHAPTER TWO

The Intelligentsia and Bread

ON SEPTEMBER 8, 1965, ON THE WAY TO A LECTURE, I WAS
arrested in the middle of a Moscow street. A first arrest is almost
like first love. You remember everything down to the smallest
details. The last words my wife said to me before I left the house
were, "Dear, we've run out of money. Maybe you could borrow
from someone until you get your salary." For many months, first
in prison and then in the camp, I agonized over what my wife and
my year-old son were eating. Where were they getting money for
bread and milk? Six years later I came home to a very rich
woman. During that time, my wife, who is an art historian, had
become a successful jewelry designer and had organized a private
business, something which at that time was virtually nonexistent. She slowly established her small workshop, where in the
evenings and on weekends two people, a physicist and a lady
architect and restorer, worked as apprentices.

In 1971 the average monthly salary of an intellectual (and the average salary in the country) was 120 rubles. A professor at Moscow State University earned 450 to 500 rubles, and my wife earned 500 to 600 and a great deal of enjoyment. Her apprentices also earned considerably more than their state salaries. After that, I started believing in the power and rationale of the private sector, and in the economic talents of my wife, Maria Vasilievna Rozanova; now we always work together on Russian economic problems.

At that time a long loaf of white bread cost thirteen kopecks, and a kilo of meat cost two rubles.

In 1973 we moved to Paris, and our lives as émigrés began. Aside from the city's architectural beauty and the long-awaited romantic encounters with the cathedral of Notre Dame and the bookstalls along the banks of the Seine, the first thing that struck us was the abundance. Food came out your ears. There were heaps of food all over the place. Soon we set off for Switzerland, and all the way there from the windows of the train we admired the beautifully tended fields and counted the cows. We began to realize that all these farms were private plots and not kolkhozes. As someone who had rather little to do with economics, I was struck by a farm where (imagine—on a single farm) there were two hundred head of cattle. What a life those people had! The writer Anatoli Gladilin told how, on the eve of his departure, his entire family had fallen ill and Sakharov lent him a chicken from his refrigerator. Gladilin had no chance to return the chicken and still has pangs of conscience about it. My wife and I sometimes did radio broadcasts for Radio Liberty, and Gladilin's story inspired us to do a broadcast called "What the Chicken Sang," by analogy with Zoshchenko's tale "What the Nightingale Sang." We spoke of the striking contrast between French abundance and Soviet poverty. Our basic point was not that everything is great in the West and bad in Russia, but rather praise for the private sector, the part of the economy that had totally disappeared in the Soviet Union.

With the beginning of perestroika, some very attractive words started flashing by: NEP (people recalled the New Economic Policy),[1] family contractors, cooperative stores, farmers, Stolypin (not the railroad cars that were then known as Stolypins, but Minister Stolypin).[2] In 1990, walking around Moscow, we became really hungry, and on Arbat Square bought a meat *pirozhok* [small filled pastry], which had been privately made. It was a fabulous *pirozhok*, made with just enough onion and just the right amount of salt and pepper. While walking down Arbat Street to Smolensk Square, we wanted to continue our acquaintance with the private sector, and we each bought another *pirozhok*. Well, my brothers and fellow citizens, that wasn't a *pirozhok*, that was a real piece of junk. It had very little meat and too much dough, and the butter was rancid. "Look, Sinyavsky," said Maria Vasilievna, "this is called competition. A good *pirozhok* brings in customers, expands production, takes over the market, and in a couple of years that *pirozhok* will turn into a Kentucky Fried Chicken. And bad *pirozhki* have got to go."

During that trip we had a wonderful meal in a cooperative

cafe. It was already quite expensive, but still affordable. A group of engineers we knew who were enthusiastic about ecological ideas organized a small firm called Ozone, which designed purification systems for industrial enterprises. I asked our friend whether he wasn't afraid of going broke, to which this novice company boss proudly answered: "Andrei Donatovich! We're producing something everyone needs. Not a single factory has the right to work unless its purification systems are in order. There are ten of us, and we'll be inundated with work." Ozone rented a wonderful Empire-style townhouse in the Arbat area from the Moscow city Soviet [i.e., the city council]. The head of the firm saw a beautiful eighteenth-century house built by Bazhenov and said dreamily: "If a part of that building were rented to Ozone we'd restore the entire house for the Moscow city Soviet." As you see, the beginning of the Gorbachev economic reforms gave people assurances about tomorrow, a sense that their work was needed, and even a bit of philanthropic spirit.

Very quickly, however, racketeers, bureaucrats, criminals, and taxes interfered with the growing buds of the new economy. The new production efforts ran into trouble. Prices shot up, the store shelves emptied, and ration coupons were imposed on many goods.

A few years later, Gorbachev admitted in his book *Perestroika*:

We missed a lot of opportunities for small business, for the agrarian sector, and for reform of the price-formation system. We couldn't regulate the market. That led to increasing dissatisfaction because the reforms did not produce tangible results.

It is true that the freedom granted in the political sphere was not paralleled by successes in the economic sphere. Even minimal success in this area would have been highly advantageous for Gorbachev by broadening the social base of perestroika. As far as the economy was concerned, Gorbachev simply acted too late. Perhaps the solution to economic problems was more complex, requiring more time and lengthy, intensive efforts. During that early period of hope and joyful expectation the majority of the population supported perestroika, but the people quickly cooled to it. They had gotten freedom but not bread. As a result Gorbachev and Yeltsin symbolized the same kind of negative force—that of ruin.

In the eyes of the people, democracy became synonymous with poverty, embezzlement of public funds, and theft. This disappointment with democracy when it has barely begun is extremely dangerous in a country without a stable democratic tradition. I recall a chance encounter in a Moscow street with a wild-looking and somewhat drunk young man wearing a cowboy hat who asked me for a light. He sadly pointed to his battered and tattered box of matches that refused to light, repeating dully, "Look at what Gorbachev's done!"

At the beginning of 1992 Yeltsin unleashed the Gaidar reforms on the country. Economic collapse began, along with the impoverishment of the population. For the first time, hungry people were visible. Do you think the flower of the nation went to their defense? Nothing of the sort!

Literaturnaya gazeta published a letter on April 12, 1992:

> Mr. President! As citizens of Russia we consider it our duty to express our firm support for the policy of radical reforms. Do not let yourself be stopped by the hysteria of temporary favorites, who, standing at the side of the road of Russian history, sense the fragility of their existence. Piotr Arkadievich Stolypin did not hesitate to put the country's welfare over reverence for parliamentary forms, forms which not a single people has ever acquired instantly. We believe that Russians support the government of the Republic. We are convinced that a direct appeal to them is an essential step. It can brook no delay.

The signatories included Zoya Krakhmalnikova, Bulat Okudzhava, and Yevgeni Pasternak.[3]

I wish to draw your attention to the intelligentsia's appeal not to feel "reverence for parliamentary forms, which not a single people has ever acquired instantly." This is a direct reference to the Supreme Soviet, where the first voices which were dissatisfied with reform were raised.

In the summer of 1992 we went to Gaidar's Moscow, and we were horrified. We had the feeling that we had returned to the wartime years of our youth, with its poverty, dirt, and miserable old women who rummaged through the dumps or brought their last worldly goods—old galoshes, junk metal, nails, screws, flowerpots, pillows—to the market. The secondhand bookstores were frightening. They had everything! I've collected books my whole life, and I've acquired a good library, but I had seen that kind of abundance only during the war, when the rarest of editions, which collectors had been actively seeking for many years, were agonizingly exchanged for bread. History was repeating itself.

We tried to talk to the Russian intelligentsia. We tried to understand its indifference to the people's misfortunes. "This is initial accumulation of capital. Things were like that throughout the world," said Yuri Ryzhov, the former provost of the Institute of Aviation, who is now the Russian ambassador to France. "In Europe there are also lots of beggars," Yuri Kariakin, now a member of the Presidential Council, answered me. "Let them sweat, let them look for things, let them sell bottles or rent their apartments," Boris Zolotukhin, the legendary lawyer who had defended dissidents and was a deputy of the Supreme Soviet (which had not yet been fired on), said with a carefree smile. "I am not an economist," Maria Chudakova, a member of the Presidential Council, proudly announced.

I am also not an economist. If you ask me what a monetary system is, I answer that I don't know. The International Monetary Fund? I don't know about that either. But I do know that economics—perhaps more than any other area of human activity—must be based on common sense.

What about the *pirozhki*, the cafes, the Ozone company? By mid-1994 we saw the end of all this petty bourgeois activity. The cooperative cafe near the movie center had closed, and there were no more *pirozhki* on the Arbat. The general director of the Ozone company lowered his eyes and, clearly embarrassed, said that he was now involved in other kinds of work. What kind? He fidgets around. Well, what kind? He doesn't want to answer. Then he admitted he was involved in *biznes*. The Western understanding of the word *business* includes a plethora of concepts, but the major thrust of *biznes* in Russia is trade—buying and selling. Our gentle friend trades in anything and everything. First it was clothing, now it's photo and film materials. He makes a decent living. And there is anguish in his eyes.

What about Ozone? What about the ten engineers and their confidence in their success? Our friend told us how the orders stopped coming in. One client dropped out and another disappeared. No one gave any reasons why. They lowered their eyes. The one client who finally agreed to talk explained everything very simply: "Why should I order a purification project from you and build it, when I can just grease the palm of the bureaucrat who gives a stamp confirming that everything is in order, and who will then sign anything and everything? He's got to live, too. And that means savings for me."

That is why I like Grigori Yavlinsky,[4] who says:

I believe that a government job should provide a man with considerable opportunities for obtaining an apartment, the comforts of life, and other such things. But if you wind up involved in corruption, that's it. Bye-bye. You bear full material responsibility. In a poor country, you cannot have people in authority living in the lap of luxury and enjoying unlimited power. Citizens can have unlimited wealth, and that's good. A businessman can also be rich, and a professor should be rich. But power cannot be unlimited. If our authorities are not modest, people will not trust them. And without the people's trust, there will be no results.

In February 1994 I brought a videotape with me to Moscow. A Swiss journalist, Teresa Obrecht, had made a documentary television film called *To Die in Moscow*. The action takes place in a cemetery, in a casino, at a market, at a railroad station, in a morgue, in the office of young businessmen, and at a city dump. It was a bitter and frightening film about how the new regime had divided the country into rich and poor. Into very rich and very poor. The main subject was how people are buried. Some of them are buried in cellophane bags (or you simply leave your father's corpse at the hospital), while others have luxurious coffins (which are given beautiful names—for example, Pushkin's Coffin). The film shows old men and women sifting through garbage dumps searching for something edible.

I tried to show this film to my Moscow friends—poets, journalists, and human rights lawyers. "We know all that," my lawyer friends objected indifferently. "Don't try to scare us! People somehow manage to get by. Nobody's died yet."

We stopped listening to our friends and started reading the newspapers. The real material. The newspapers also write about death. Poverty is so extreme that in a newspaper you see an appeal to "Help bury someone!"

In 1992, we lost all of our savings in the devaluation. Mama's condition has deteriorated. She literally has one foot in the grave. There's just enough money for food. We need fruit because of her kidney problems, there's not enough money for our son's medicine, or to repair old shoes, or for the hairdresser. But the major problem will be the funeral. Mama wants a Christian burial, with a church service. Help me, tell me where can I get money for the funeral?

(*Nezavisimaya gazeta*, August 30, 1994)

Here is an excerpt from *Moskovsky komsomolets*:

Seven half-decayed corpses are lying right out in the street, sprawled in the sunshine. The bodies are covered with a polyethylene sheet, and their bare legs stick out. For a radius of thirty meters there is such a smell you could go crazy. A swarm of enormous green flies circles over this whole gloomy landscape. The corpses lie under the wall of the wretched one-story morgue in the Mytishchinskaya Central Regional Hospital, the only one for a hundred kilometers. The food service center for the hospital is also located here. The flies, naturally, are shared by both buildings. Next door is a residential five-story house. People live there . . .

"Where am I going to put them?" asked the chief doctor of the hospital, annoyed by the journalist's question. "These corpses are unclaimed, they're full of lice, and they're under investigation. They can't be buried without permission from the police . . . What are you surprised at? This doesn't only happen here. Go to Pushkino. Go see the hospitals in the provinces."

Enough about the dead. Let's talk about the living. A journalist from the newspaper *Vek* (which is certainly not an opposition newspaper) got hold of an extraordinary document, a notebook listing the expenditures of Tamara Ivanovna, a sixty-year-old retired widow living in the Moscow region, in which she recorded her daily expenses. How does a retiree draw up her budget?

Her pension is 141,000 rubles a month. Medicines account for 10,000; toothpaste, 2,000; household soap, 2,800; bath soap, 1,500; a box of the cheapest laundry detergent, 5,000; stamps for two letters, 3,200. The rent, radio, and electricity use up another 30,000. Ninety thousand remains for food. How is it possible to live on this when the minimum food basket in the Moscow area costs 188,767 rubles?

Tamara Ivanovna tells us how. She buys 200 grams of butter a month and one can of processed meat spread. If she puts a teaspoon of the meat spread into a meatless soup the can will last for twenty days. A dozen eggs. Fifteen loaves of black bread a month at 2,000 rubles a loaf. White bread is a delicacy; she can't afford more than three loaves. A package of tea costs 3,000. A bucket of potatoes a month costs 15,000 rubles. There's no money for other vegetables (let alone fruit). A bottle of vegetable oil costs 10,000 rubles. Tamara Ivanovna's diet contains no fruit, meat, fish, sausage, or dairy products. Candy, jam, and cookies all remain in the Communist past. A note in this sad financial diary regrets that "For the rest of my life, going to the movies, visiting museums, and other forms of cultural entertainment will be unaffordable. . . . Seeing friends is also a thing of the past. Guests are now an expensive pleasure" (*Vek*, November 17, 1995).

> The average unemployment benefit is now about 200,000 rubles. The subsistence wage, however, has already exceeded 300,000 rubles, and in the northern regions is half a million. Nearly half of the unemployed can claim only the minimum benefits: 70,000 to 80,000 rubles, sums at which even bread becomes a delicacy and a luxury. "We mostly eat animal fodder. For breakfast, lunch, and dinner." This was said by several unemployed people.
>
> (*Vek*, November 17, 1995)

> We remember how our president threatened to lie down on the railroad tracks if the promised improvements did not take place. But it looks as though we are the ones who will have to do that, in order to finally draw his attention to our problems and to make him see that the only changes that have taken place are changes for the worse.
>
> (*Izvestia*, March 1, 1996)

Perhaps I'm reverting to my childhood, but I'm sitting here cutting up newspapers, the way I did when I was small. In those happy times I cut out pictures. Today I cut out howls of despair. What emerges is an interminable tale of hopelessness and the end of the world. Hunger, unemployment, a drop in the level of production (I have a set of clippings about that, too), what next? Then that frightening word *demography* appears, and it is clear that Russia today is on the eve of a demographic catastrophe: the death rate is exceeding the birthrate, life expectancy is declining sharply, the number of suicides is rising, and there are 240 abortions per 100 live births.

I began this chapter by telling about our Radio Liberty broadcast "What the Chicken Sang," devoted to the difficult material situation of the Soviet people. Today the Soviet production setbacks of the seventies seem laughable. And disastrous. Disastrous for the hungry people, disastrous for the egoistic intellectual elite, for my friend the priest, with whom I had a rather remarkable conversation. He asked how I liked the new Moscow construction projects, the Iversk gates on Red Square and the cathedral of Christ the Savior. I tried to appeal to his religious feelings, saying that when there was such catastrophic poverty, all these government building projects looked somewhat blasphemous, like the Stalinist "great building projects of communism." My friend calmly replied that there have always been paupers in Russia and that paupers go (i.e., they die) and churches remain. Another intellectual argued heatedly with me, saying, "These paupers have more money than you and I!" I told of seeing my wife leaving the bakery and giving the loaf she had bought to an old woman who was asking for bread. I was interrupted by laughter: "That old woman went off to sell the loaf at a profit!" No, that woman started eating it greedily then and there.

They were talking about lofty and eternal questions, and I was talking about plain, ordinary things, about bread, about things many of my friends for some reason don't want to know and don't want to think about. Why? One answer came from the journalist Aleksandr Borodynia who used the repulsive words *used to it*.

> For around two years, I worked in TV at the crime desk. I saw the worst: murders and blood. I've seen more than my share of real blood. First it made me sick. Now I find myself calmly gazing at the corpses of two little girls killed by their own mother. I find that now I'm indifferent. I don't reject this mass of horrendous events; I'm becoming used to it.

"What should the people do?" I ask. "Let them hustle, let them squirm, let them sell bottles, they're used to having everything handed to them, they're used to hanging on the government's neck." That is the reproach of the intelligentsia to people who fail to show any initiative. But people sometimes do show initiative.

> In Saratov, 52-year-old Yuri Lukin was found guilty of swindling and was sentenced by the city court to two years' imprisonment in a strict-regime labor camp, a 50,000-ruble fine, and compulsory treatment for alcoholism. Six months ago, while working as a guard, Lukin got drunk, went to the pathology laboratory of the morgue of the

Railroad Clinical Hospital, took from a metal container about three kilos of human organs which had been removed during operations, and sold them at the local market, saying they were ordinary meat.

(IMA press, October 12, 1994)

We started "going to the people," first to the Moscow markets, and then to the provinces. We saw that there were fewer Russian products, and that the markets were flooded with very familiar fruits and vegetables.

We asked one seller, "Where are the eggplants from?" "Germany." We asked another: "Where's the red pepper from?" "Holland." "Where are the roses from?" "Ecuador."

"What kind of apples are these?" my wife asked. "Golden." "Do Golden apples grow in Russia?" "They're from Holland." "So there are no more Russian apples?" "How can we have apples when we're busy howling or demonstrating? Besides, it's hard to ship them." "So it's easier to bring them from Holland?" my wife kept on. "Lady, you just don't understand!" the vendor exploded. "I'll sell these apples and there will be two fewer unemployed people in Holland, and nobody gives a damn about our own unemployed people!" I was surprised. How come that ordinary man had so much common sense?

In the provinces things were even worse. We were returning to Moscow from Belarus on the old Smolensk road, and all along the way people were standing by the roadside holding pots. What were they doing in the midst of the forest? Where had they come from? They were workers from a pot factory who had not been paid their salaries for several months. Instead, they were paid in kind, in enamel pots.

The newspaper *Trud* reported on June 23, 1994:

Not all the skilled workers of the Gus-Khrustalnyi plants believe in the theory of Karl Marx, but every single worker lives by his immortal formula: goods-money-goods. The Russian authorities are forcing them to do that. Since they do not receive their salaries regularly, they are managing to get the results of their labor to the market. These "results" today are their salaries. The best crystal in our country is probably most popular with people who are traveling through these areas. It's good that there are plenty of railroad stations, and that there are a lot of travelers driving along the roads to these places. As soon as a train or a bus comes to a halt you hear the gentle clink of wine glasses, champagne flutes, and crystal salad bowls. Multicolored glass horses and other wonderful glass objects seem to say, "Buy us—we're so pretty and so cheap."

And the travelers? They buy these things, and that allows these skilled workers to make ends meet: to sell their talent, to earn money, to buy sausage, potatoes, bread, clothes, and shoes. People are living the way they did during the times of medieval markets.

The newspaper *Moskovsky komsomolets* chose a somewhat more spicy subject, and told of how Vologda loggers were paid their salary in female sanitary napkins. Fellow passengers on the Moscow-Karaganda train told us how in Karaganda workers were paid in vodka—and the results. In one place workers were paid in bras, in another in fabric, and workers on the collective farm near Staraya Russa in the Novgorod oblast were paid in calves.

Sociologists of the Public Opinion Foundation analyzed the results of a survey of the Russian urban and rural population (1,370 respondents) and concluded that in no region aside from Moscow and St. Petersburg did the number of respondents who lived better under capitalism exceed the number of those who chose socialism. In the Povolzhe area the ratio of those who preferred socialism to the capitalist future was nearly seven to one: 68 percent and 10 percent, respectively.

Only in Moscow and St. Petersburg was the majority of respondents (59 percent) opposed to a return to the "era of stagnation." In other cities and towns, and in all regions of the country, there were more supporters than opponents of a restoration of the old system (*Obshchaya gazeta*, April 27, 1995).

We can use a few newspaper headlines to illustrate today's tragedy in Russia:

Life Is Good Now—You've Got Things to Look At and to Sniff

In Ballet and Vodka We Lead the Entire Planet

October Inflation Rate, 104.7%—the Rate for the Year So Far, 214.4%

Stand in Line Until You Die

Poverty Is Tragic Not Because of the Lack of Money, but Because of the Loss of Dignity

Teachers: Our Poverty Has Reached the Limit

The State's Debt to Workers Has Doubled: 11.5 Trillion Rubles in Salaries Has Not Been Paid

The Fall in the Russian Standard of Living Continues

The Collection of Funds from Privatization Is a Failure

No Work, No Money, No Bread for Thousands of People in the Far East Today

5,847 Strikes in Our Country Since the Beginning of the Year

Our Prices for Butter, Sugar, and Gas Are Higher Than World Prices

Boris Yeltsin Intends to Halt Capital Flight

Fewer and Fewer Cradles: Russia Is on the Eve of a Demographic Catastrophe

Russian Shoes Have Worn Out During the Reforms

The notices and advertisements in the newspapers also tell us a lot and show the country's turmoil. Anything and everything is bought and sold, but some things are especially popular. For example, "vicious puppies from vicious parents" are in particular demand. Hand-to-hand combat is taught at the School for Survival. There is an ad for a driver who knows karate, or for a driver-bodyguard. Girls seeking jobs as cashiers sometimes add "no intimate situations"—and sometimes don't. Somebody is selling "four wheels from a child's carriage," or "two packages of cotton." People are selling their last possessions.

You can tell how people live by the songs they sing. We were amazed to hear the words of a refrain to a song: "Poverty, my poverty." It sounded almost like "Shagane, my Shagane."[5] The intellectuals hummed a tune, though they did not quite understand what they were singing about:

> Better be full than hungry,
> Better live in peace than in strife,
> Better be needed than be free,
> That's the way I feel.

"Better be needed than be free." It sounds, I would say, sadly cynical. What we see now on center stage is the idea of being needed and even recruited. That idea is gaining ground. That is better than death from hunger.

The intelligentsia as well as the people are suffering, and so are science and art, which are experiencing difficult times in this ravaged country. At a recent conference in Moscow the elderly academician V. B. Raushenbakh (born in 1915) lamented:

> Our leadership today is totally indifferent to what Russia will be like twenty years from now. They cannot see any further than their own noses, two or three years ahead. In the past things were different. Take the year 1918. Though the

situation in the country was worse than it is today, Lenin organized scientific centers such as the Central Aerohydro-dynamics Institute and the Physics Technical Institute in St. Petersburg, which gave us Nobel Prize laureates such as Kapitsa and Semenov, the leader of our nuclear program, Kurchatov, and many other scientists. Lenin looked ahead. Or take the horrible era of Stalin, who, while mercilessly destroying individual scholars, continued to provide financing for science. Scientists who had been shot were replaced by others. Despite the Stalinist terror, science as a whole moved forward. Stalin also looked to the future. Today our scientists are forced to go to the West because here they're simply not allowed to work. Never mind the humiliatingly small salary; the purchases of equipment or the reagents they need are not being financed, and experimental facilities are not being created. To sum up, everything is being done to prevent scientific work in our country.

Stanislav Govorukhin[6] echoed these thoughts:

Do you remember our revolutionary Fifth Congress of Cinematographers? Just give us freedom, we demanded, and we need nothing more. You don't even need to subsidize us, we'll manage. What happened? What were the results? They abolished the shelf of forbidden films. Yet, as became clear later, the majority of the films lying on that shelf were not in fact banned for ideological reasons. For the most part, those piles of films were things nobody wanted.

That became clear when they were taken out into the light of day. What happened? That shelf remained, and now there are many more films lying on it. Only one film of mine, *The Great Criminal Revolution*, was never shown for political reasons. The rest are there because in the heat of battle we managed to destroy the very best thing that we had in cinematography, the countrywide system of distributing and renting out films. Then you could see a film in any village, at any weather station. Now the two-hundred-odd films produced by Russian cinematographers have for practical purposes ended up on the shelf, because they do not get to the public. We have created a new phenomenon: movies without an audience. We began as revolutionaries and ended as a firing squad, as horrendous reactionaries.

(Quoted in Gorbachev's Perestroika)

But not everyone is so badly off. The hope of our intelligentsia—the new class—is growing. Almost as described by Djilas.[7] This new class has its own amusements.

The staff of the Green Grove Sochi vacation center has set up a business at Stalin's dacha here. They've reassembled stolen furniture, and with the help of reminiscences of eyewitnesses have restored the interiors and placed a figure of the genius of mankind in the living room; it was produced and assembled at a cost of seven million rubles. "They brought in the pieces of the wax figure and assembled it right here," said comrade Shishkin, the deputy director of the vacation center. "Now our guests can have their photos taken standing next to the figure. Iosif Vissarionovich will pay for himself very quickly."

The apartments are occupied by distinguished individuals, businessmen, statesmen, and other affluent clients. The prices are affordable. For example, [as of March 1995] a night in Stalin's daughter Svetlana's bedroom cost only 360,000 rubles. And how many impressions you get for that!

The most expensive apartments at the dacha cost half a million rubles a day. That's without meals. With meals, medical treatment, etc., they cost about a million. The clients are regulars. They come with their families. An article entitled "A Night Alone with Stalin" reported that some very important state functions take place at the dacha. They say that Stalin's rooms are conducive to clear thinking and that important questions can be resolved there quickly and without red tape. Perhaps that is why the All-Russian meeting of regional representatives of the President took place here.

(*Komsomolskaya Pravda*, March 15, 1995, quoting from V. Pisigin)

The Izhevsk firm Gambit offers well-off inhabitants and guests of the city of Izhevsk a party behind barbed wire.

The director of the firm reported that an excursion into the prison zone, located in the village of Karakalai, is planned for potential partners of the defense complex enterprises.

After tense negotiations they can relax in a casual atmosphere. Tourists get to try prison grub, have a chat with the young prison trustees, and are photographed in prison garb. More sophisticated dishes are planned for those who don't care for camp rations. The cost of a weekend is $500. The first group of fans of such exotic prison fare has already been assembled.

(*Trud*, October 18, 1994)

Permission has been given at the testing ground around Krasnoarmeisk for so-called war tours. Now those willing to pay can practice shooting an armor-piercing shell at moving and stationary targets from a T-80 tank. Or they can shoot off cannon, self-propelled guns, grenade-launchers, or flamethrowers.

It costs $300 for one shot from a Hyacinth artillery launcher and $500 for one from a T-80 tank. Any target can be arranged. They can set up a shield for you with a tank drawn on it, or an old or decrepit tank or an armored personnel carrier. All you have to do is pay. I think that for those sums, there would be no lack of clients even for living targets. Just advertise!

(*Moskovsky komsomolets*, December 2, 1994)

Four years have passed since the Gaidar reforms, and it is now perfectly clear that these reforms have failed. Today Gaidar and his team of intellectuals are trying to prove that were it not for the reforms, the country would have starved. "Don't you remember the empty store shelves?" they ask. "When there was milk only for two or three hours, we didn't always have bread, cheese was nonexistent, and many goods were sold only for ration coupons? You were in Moscow then." Yes, we remember. We remember everything very well. For some reason, however, our opponents have totally forgotten about the new criminal organizations, and that goods, once they leave the producers' gates, never get to the consumer. This was the first alarm bell warning us that Soviet criminals were also busy preparing for market reform and for shock therapy.

None of Gaidar's current defenders and lovers of the word *defitsit* [shortage] want to understand that shortages can be created in two ways. The first is by depriving the consumer of goods. The second is by depriving him of money. In the final analysis, the result is the same.

Yet another comment. While it is true that prior to Gaidar there were empty shelves in the stores, there were also markets where everything was sold at three times the store price. Three times as expensive, my opponents exclaim, instead of making the very simple calculation that, relative to the average salary, during the Gorbachev era milk bought at the market was cheaper than milk bought today in the store.

Finally, and most important, such fateful reforms cannot be carried out by a man who changes his professional views as he would change his gloves. In August 1989 he opposed private property and the market, favoring solely "a policy of the renewal of socialism, including the democratization of public life and . . .

the development of a system of social guarantees." Unfortunately, intellectuals have short memories, and they do not reread old newspapers. That was a quotation from Gaidar's article in *Moskovskie novosti*.

Spiteful people say that the nice, socialist boy Gaidar was taught bad things by bad guys from America such as Anders Aslund and Jeffrey Sachs.[8] I don't know either of them, and perhaps these are malicious rumors. But in talking about the ads and names plastered everywhere we have already mentioned the increasingly anti-American mood in Russia.

The democrats have let their opportunity slip. I don't like the Communists, but they are better for the people than the democrats. It is not fortuitous that the very word *democrat* has been compromised and that people call democrats "demo-thieves." Democracy is associated with poverty, theft, corruption, and other horrors. Against that background the Communists look wonderful. People either don't remember what happened in the past or say, "Well, they've changed for the better, they'll correct their mistakes."

I think that an intellectual doesn't always have to want what the people want. After all, the people wanted Hitler, but was the intelligentsia supposed to want him, too? In the case of the Communists the problem is that there is no money, and people want to eat. For Russia, of course, the symbol of money has always been America. Perhaps America won't give us money if the Communists win, or it will depend on how the Communists behave. I hope America doesn't give us any money if people are

once agai
work he
Americ
I rec
writer
Engli
shop'
stud
they
rec
th
a

CHAPTER THREE

The Intelligentsia and Democracy

WE HAD BEEN LIVING IN FRANCE FOR SEVEN YEARS WHEN another round of lengthy transportation and mail strikes took place, seriously inconveniencing everyone. Walking to work, waiting for hours in the jammed subway, and going for weeks without letters and newspapers is not much fun. At one point I started loudly grumbling and complaining about the French system in the presence of my fifteen-year-old son. I said that I thought that people in professions such as communications and transportation, police, and medicine should be barred from striking and should be obliged to sign contracts to that effect. Otherwise the entire life of the country would collapse. My young son strongly objected. "Papa," he said, "don't you understand that a right is a right only because it is an equal right for everybody? If it's not granted to everyone then it's no longer a right but a privilege."

I felt slightly ashamed. My son is a good deal more French than I. Despite my democratic feelings and inclinations, every now and then vestiges of Soviet habits probably show through in me. In any case, my little son taught me a lesson in democracy.

At the end of 1994 the poet Iunna Moritz was asked what concerned her most in today's world. "The need to survive rather than to live," she answered. "The substitution of surviving for living is poisoning people. If laws do not function in a country, then nothing in that country has changed." And nothing has changed, although democracy was proclaimed in Russia long ago.

Remember August 1991. Yeltsin, Rutskoi, and Khasbulatov are on those democratic tanks in front of the White House. General exultation. In Paris we get a call from Moscow from the poet Andrei Chernov, who shouts, "Congratulate us! We're finally free! We've become Europeans!" Just for a moment it seemed that democracy was really victorious in Russia, and that Soviet slavery was a thing of the past. But very soon people began to have their doubts.

On November 15, 1991, an editorial in the émigré journal *Sintaksis* stated:

Three days of a coup, three days of euphoria, and then the doubts began. Had the democrats really won? How much more progressive is the Sverdlovsk mafia than the Dnepropetrovsk mafia? Can you loot what has already been looted? Aren't these questions produced by the very nature

of the Soviet state, which, even while collapsing, can repro-
duce itself again and again?

In this book I preface many of my views with references to
dusty newspapers. Going through piles of newspapers from the
last three years I discovered that although the country was con-
tinually getting stuck while building a democracy imbued with
capitalism, some minds in Russia are still functioning. Not everyone has gone mad. Not everyone has succumbed to collective
lunacy. The farther you move away from the troubled years of
1991 and 1993, the clearer the writings of those analysts who
were not blinded by the instincts of the herd, who were not
afraid of expressing unfashionable views and making their own
predictions, which turned out to be justified. We at the journal
Sintaksis were determined that these texts, along with other
excellent ones, not be forgotten. That is why we shall regularly
republish them, imitating the elderly poet Derzhavin. Remember: "And old man Derzhavin noticed us."[1] We also believe that
free thinking must be rewarded. Today there are so many fash-
ionable prizes: the Swedish Nobel Prize, the American Pulitzer
Prize, the British-Russian Booker Prize, the Odessa Golden
Duke. We are making our contribution by establishing the annual
Cassandra Prize for sober views, independent thinking, and
accurate political forecasting. After lengthy debates, the
Cassandra jury (to which Pushkin and Lermontov and the
Marquis de Custine were invited)[2] awarded the Cassandra Prize
to Dmitri Furman of Moscow.

This is what Furman predicted on September 3, 1991, in *Nezavisimaya gazeta*:

The putsch of August 19 and the simultaneous heroic defense of the White House seem to have given a green light for everything. Once again newspapers are closing (now nondemocratic ones), and disloyal local authorities are being removed. In the Russian Parliament a new (and yet very ancient) spirit is triumphant, the spirit of "applause becoming an ovation." The victory of the democrats is becoming a serious threat to democracy, and there are clear signs that an authoritarian regime is developing, headed by a leader, a "popular president," with a democratic movement devoted to him. Its ideology and symbolism are dominated by anticommunism, Russian nationalism, and nationalistically tinged orthodoxy.

Democracy is not the rule of the party of the democrats, in particular our democrats. Democracy is the struggle of parties within the framework of the law. Now the democrats have virtually no opposition because the Communist party has collapsed. But if the democrats do not need the opposition, democracy needs it as the air we breathe. We do not need to rally around Yeltsin and dance on the bones of a defeated opponent. We need criticism of a democracy in which the idea of democracy is increasingly being replaced by the idea of a Greater Russia, a Yeltsin kingdom arising on the shards of the Soviet Union. We need a closing of the ranks of all those who are frightened by this prospect, who place democracy above party interests, and whose interests do not clash with to the principles of democracy, but who oppose this specific incarnation of democracy. If that does not happen, no matter how much we talk about democracy we shall again end up with totalitarianism, which will return in a new and therefore unrecognized form, the same way there was a sudden, unexpected return—not from the Whites but from the Bolsheviks, in highly intensified form—of the worst evils of autocracy.

I again stress that these words were written two weeks after the putsch, when everyone was ecstatic over Yeltsin's victory and when Dmitri Furman had no supporters. He was alone against everyone. Incidentally, Vitali Tretyakov, the editor of *Nezavisimaya gazeta*, also displayed moral courage by publishing this seditious material even though, at the time, he did not agree with it.

But Furman did not calm down. On October 8, 1991, he wrote in *Nezavisimaya gazeta*:

A mechanism for punishing breaches of morality seems to exist in history. A new kind of authoritarianism is the inevitable price paid by revolution for its sins and blindness. For us, too, that coming authoritarianism will be a punishment for the fact that in our country the struggle for the principles of democracy was replaced by a struggle against the center of the Soviet Union and the Communist party; punishment because we were ready to elect any scoundrel a deputy as long as he declared himself a democrat and anticommunist; punishment for our abuse of the man who did more than anyone for Russian democracy, Gorbachev (and we enjoyed our own pseudocourage, knowing in the depth of our hearts that this was perfectly safe because he was not a vindictive person and was losing power). It will be our punishment for having taken advantage of the failure of the putsch in order to bring down the Soviet Union once and for all without giving any thought to the consequences, including the consequences for newborn Russian democracy.

In the November 1991 issue of the journal *Vek XX i mir*, Furman sums up:

What will happen later is more or less clear—a new authoritarian system headed by Yeltsin, who cannot be blamed for anything, because he is being carried along by a wave of history that has caught him, raced through the democratic-populist stage, and is now pushing him toward the role of "Grand Prince," who relies on the democratic movement that is devoted to him and that is increasingly dominated by rhetorical anticommunism and Russian nationalism. As in 1917, the cycle of this revolution is going from authoritarianism to a new authoritarianism or totalitarianism, skipping over the stage of democracy and rejecting the "indecisive" Miliukovs, Kerenskys, and Gorbachevs.[3]

I have virtually no doubt that in the near future such people as Nevzorov[4] will understand that Yeltsin is in fact the new Russian czar for whom they longed, and the idealists remaining in the democratic camp will be kicked out. In their kitchens (we hope it will be in their kitchens) they will joke, "Well, you got what you wanted."

Having given due credit to *Sintaksis* and its prizewinner Dmitri Furman, let us ask the age-old Russian question "Who is to blame?"

Today my answer is the intelligentsia and autocracy. Let us recall Soviet history. From very early on comrade Lenin fought against czarism. He won. In the final analysis, and without wanting to do it, he established autocracy, the rule of one party and its leader, i.e., the party's czar.

In 1921 one of the eminent Communist-Leninists, Adolf Ioffe, wrote a letter to Lenin complaining that the Central Committee of the party was Lenin's autocratic "ego." Astounded, Lenin responded that this accusation was entirely the result of Ioffe's nervous exhaustion and that he was in dire need of medical treatment. By 1921, however, Lenin could have said, "I am the Central Committee," and, like Louis XIV, "L'état c'est moi!" Of course, the formula "I am the state" was not uttered, but the theory behind it was worked out and put into practice by Lenin himself. Lenin provided a scientific (I stress—scientific!) formulation of Soviet state power. "The scientific concept of the dictatorship," asserted Lenin, "means nothing else than unlimited power, bound by no laws or rules, and directly based on violence."

Lenin was an unusual czar. He was a czar who did not want anything for himself personally and who worked sixteen-hour days, involving himself in every detail of the state machinery he was setting up. At the same time, reading the last few volumes of Lenin's collected works, the endless telegrams, corrections, and instructions regarding all kinds of problems coming directly from Lenin (down to who should be arrested and who should be released from prison), one is amazed at the cumbersome and awkward state apparatus he founded. People fear to make decisions because they are waiting to see what the great specialist on the state system—Lenin—is going to say. They come crawling to him for instructions on anything and everything, and he comes right back with instructions on each and every issue. Everything depends on the czar. He must be involved in everything and act on everything. Lenin was involved and kept giving orders although he was practically on his deathbed.

Moscow mediums recently called up Lenin's spirit and congratulated him on the Communist victory in the Duma elections. Lenin answered, or more precisely knocked, saying that from his point of view Zyuganov was not a Communist. The real Communists will be people born at the beginning of the twenty-first century. Then, Lenin said encouragingly, there will be no bloodshed. Lenin was very reluctant to continue these contacts, however, and was not very talkative.

Many years have passed. The czar is long gone, Lenin is gone, and democracy has been proclaimed. In a recent interview with the newspaper *Sobesednik* (January 1996), the writer Anatoli Pristavkin said:

In Russia everything hinges on one person, his authority, his personality, his strength and real power. Yeltsin in fact had that. He kept on behaving like the "boss." The most important thing is that the people accept this. The fact that everything hinges on one individual who must resolve questions ranging from matchboxes to outer space—that means a huge workload. This is not because the President wanted it, but because we cannot act any other way.

How similar to Lenin!

Lenin's successor Stalin understood the nature of power perfectly, in particular the nature of state power in Russia. Even more openly than Lenin, he based his art of governing and ruling on the ancient Russian tradition of autocracy. Soon after Lenin's death, at a party dinner, Stalin let slip a comment that Russia needed a czar. "Don't forget," said Stalin, "that we are living in Russia, the country of the czars. The Russian people like it when one single individual heads the state." No one then paid attention to that comment. Yet this idea, which was a strange notion for a Communist, became a reality, and on an incredible scale. Stalin fused the Leninist tradition of centralized and unlimited power based on violence with the monarchist tradition. Stalin had learned from Russia's past that the Russian czar must be terrible and even frightening. At the same time he must occasionally, as the ultimate favor, deign to bestow a smile on the people. It is not fortuitous that at the height of the repressions of the thirties, when villages were impoverished, Stalin tossed out a slogan to the people: "Life has become better, comrades! Life has become more joyous!" The country took up Stalin's smile with happy songs. An old revolutionary, Olitskaya, a member of the Socialist Revolutionary party who spent nearly her entire life under Soviet power in prison, tells how, under Stalin, she was being transported with young women Communists in a prison railroad car. While going through the depths of Siberia to a camp, the old prisoner was amazed to hear these newly arrived women prisoners singing with selfless sincerity, "I know of no other country where a man can breathe so free."[5] We could call this Stalinist hypnosis, which had spread all over Russia.

Stalin's bloodthirstiness and odd behavior somewhat resembled the terrible czar. In her memoirs Stalin's daughter Svetlana asserts that in 1952 her father "twice asked the new membership of the Central Committee to allow him to resign. They all chorused that this was impossible. Did he expect any other answers from this harmonious chorus?" Svetlana asked. "And did he in fact want to resign? This is reminiscent of the ruses of Ivan the Terrible who would go off to a monastery complaining of old age and fatigue and order the boyars to select a new czar."

Stalin's similarity to Ivan the Terrible and to other royal relics make today's nationalists and even the Communists adore him. Under Stalin, they sigh, there was real order.

Near the end of his life Stalin said benevolently to one of his minor associates, Nikolai Bulganin:[6] "Ah, Kolya! I'm going to die. You'll all be done for without me." Stalin's foreboding may have been absolutely correct, but it is hard to determine precisely whom he had in mind—the narrow circle of future leaders, the Communist party, or his own great and frightening empire? We are still feeling the reverberations from Stalin's life and personality.

Though the democrats naturally cannot stand either Lenin or Stalin, something forces them to cling to the figure of another leader, though perhaps not as authoritarian as in the past. When Yeltsin said there can be no alternative to himself, the democrats joyously agreed. For several years now we have been hearing this incantation: "There is no alternative! There is no alternative!" It sounded particularly frightening after the firing on the White House when a large part of the intelligentsia supported Yeltsin. The major argument of our opponents was once again the assumption that democratic Russia allegedly had no alternative to Yeltsin, and that Yeltsin was the only incarnation of democracy in Russia. If Yeltsin had not fired on the White House, either the Communists and fascists would have come to power or a civil war would have begun. In other words, they are proposing the lesser of two evils.

I categorically disagree with this kind of logic. When the choice is only between two evils, good is no longer an option. Then human thought and freedom disappear.

I found an unexpected kindred spirit upon reading Stanislav Govorukhin's statement in an interview:

Foreign correspondents once said to me, "You must agree that there is no alternative to Yeltsin." I answered, "Let's go look out the window." This was in my apartment. I went to the window and, wouldn't you know it, there was no one outside. Then some guy with a mesh shopping bag walked by. "Hey, look," I said, "there's an alternative to Yeltsin. Let's go ask him. I'm sure he was never a member of the Politburo. It's quite possible he doesn't drink. That means he's no worse."

Frankly speaking, when I'm asked publicly whether there is an alternative to Yeltsin, I always say: "Yes, there is. Any of you is an alternative to Yeltsin. It couldn't be worse. You simply couldn't think of anyone worse." Like Gaidar, Yeltsin for me was always a kind of composite image.

Two misfortunes are killing Russia and perestroika: autocracy in general and the intelligentsia in particular, because it cannot rid itself of the vestiges of autocratic thinking. The press accounts of a meeting of the intelligentsia in Moscow's Central Literary Center on March 18, 1993, were very revealing. "The seventh Congress woke up the president," Vyacheslav Kostikov[7] declared at the meeting.

At yesterday's meeting of the Presidential Council he was the way I remember him in August 1991. He fully agreed with all the appeals from the Council to act decisively, and he is ready to do his duty to Russia and for the reforms.

The writers' meeting was dominated by support for direct presidential rule. It is interesting that the writers expressed more radical views than did politicians such as Galina Starovoitova,[8] who emphasized the need for guarantees for further democratic development. The statement by Timur Gaidar (Yegor Gaidar's father) was also interesting. Emphasizing that he was expressing a purely personal opinion, he proposed direct presidential rule for a strictly limited period of time (Radio Ekho Moskvy, March 18, 1993). This was practically a paraphrase of what Krylov had written, "The czar, they cry, the czar! They've come with the czar."[9]

A comment about the Russian soul. I hear it rather often said that by having fired on the Supreme Soviet, Yeltsin finally crushed the power of the Soviets—that Soviet power we all hate. This view reflects a blind reverence for words, a trait particularly characteristic of Russians. Words are understood too literally and eclipse the real meaning of a phenomenon. No one remembers now that the Soviets never played a substantive role in the Soviet state. The Soviets represented a purely formal aspect of that state authority, in which the leading role was played not so much by the party as by the narrow party elite in the form of the Politburo and its leader, the czar. The Supreme Soviet that was fired on was the first parliament in seventy-five years that had dared to speak with its own voice. Neither czar Boris nor the Russian intelligentsia liked that voice of the people. A few days after the firing on the White House, Yeltsin removed the sentries from the Lenin Mausoleum, thereby throwing a symbolic bone to the intelligentsia: "Look, Soviet power has ended with those Kremlin sentries at the coffin." All this, however—the Soviets and the sentries—is merely window dressing. The real issue is that of autocratic power without any kind of control by the Parliament. That is why at the dawn of Soviet history the Russian philosopher Georgi Fedotov asserted that "new Soviet man has not merely been molded in the Marxist school; he arrived in God's world from the kingdom of Muscovy."[10]

Yet another comment. When I speak about the lust for power of today's intelligentsia and of its guilt before the people, I am referring only to the privileged part of the intelligentsia, what I call the court and government intelligentsia: people who are well known. From the very first days of perestroika these chosen few in Moscow exerted a tremendous influence on people's minds. A great deal was given them, and that is why today I am asking a great deal of them. While welcoming the idea of perestroika and Gorbachev's innovations, the elite sounded off in irate articles about the accursed times of Stalinism and stagnation. It was interested only in itself and tried to find solutions only to its own problems.

When Bulat Okudzhava came to Paris he said to me, "I disagree with you." I asked him why. "In Russia, there is no democracy, and maybe there never will be," he said. "But I support Yeltsin for two reasons. First, I'm being published without censorship. Second, I can go to the West, I can give concerts and make money." I have the most friendly feelings for Okudzhava. I like him as a friend, as a poet, as a prose writer. But just imagine if Leo Tolstoy or

Chekhov had said, "I support the czar because he doesn't bother me. I can put up with the censorship. He lets me travel." It is unthinkable for an intellectual to make a statement like that. Unthinkable. That is why I'm stressing this. After all, the dissidents started with Okudzhava and his songs. His words smack of ordinary individual cynicism, but that was followed by public cynicism, social cynicism, and then the intellectual elite reached out for power. Why? I believe it was for one purpose: to make use of power—when needed—like a policeman: to demand that one or another unsuitable newspaper be closed, or to protect the singer Kobzon from the journalists.[11] They seem to have forgotten the old rule recently referred to by the writer Andrei Bitov:[12]

> The intelligentsia is the intelligentsia precisely because it keeps its distance from power. . . . I do not understand why the intelligentsia should come close to any kind of power. . . . The intelligentsia is helpless because it is impossible to force someone to understand who does not understand, and because cooperation with that power can lead to a loss of self. Therefore one can and should express one's point of view in print, in public, or in any other way. But I do not see ways for cooperating with power.
>
> *Literaturnaya gazeta*, February 28, 1996

Those intellectuals who came to power and began cooperating with the authorities proved capable of working only for their own interests. The authorities make use of these intellectuals as they see fit, as a respectable cover-up that looks like democracy.

In arguing here with these subcontractors to the authorities I in no way wish to offend the thousands of utterly devoted intellectuals scattered throughout the schools, plants, libraries, and hospitals of the capital and the provinces, towns and cities, villages, and settlements. This group, which I call the grassroots intelligentsia, remains virtually silent and speechless; it is not guilty before the people and bears no responsibility for the sins committed by the high-ranking elite.

The war in Chechnya shook Yeltsin's prestige. A number of well-known individuals, including the human rights champion Sergei Kovalev, left the Presidential Council. In an open letter to the president that sounds almost like a criminal indictment, Kovalev stated:

> Your policy today can only very quickly re-create a state bordering on lawlessness. You swore to build a state of the people and for the people, and instead you built a bureaucratic pyramid on top of the people and opposed to the people. Some naive individuals still think it is the democrats who have power in the Kremlin. Your policy has compromised that very word.

When Kovalev was asked whether the war in Chechnya was not in fact a continuation of the firing on the White House, he answered that these events were implicitly rather than explicitly linked. In the past, Kovalev had firmly supported the firing on the White House. This made me particularly indignant, because it was precisely the blood of the White House that gave Yeltsin the freedom to wage war in Chechnya. Here I see a thoroughly explicit rather than implicit link.

Only four people left the Presidential Council; other members, including the director Mark Zakharov, the writer Daniil Granin, and the philologist Marietta Chudakova, hastened to distance themselves from Kovalev. They were frightened by the victory of the Communists in the Duma and clutched at the president like a drowning man at a straw. "The President remains the major bulwark of democracy in Russia, and the guarantor of its constitution. This unquestioned fact is now particularly important because of the vastly greater threat of a Bolshevik restoration" (*Izvestia*, February 7, 1996).

Voices in those circles ask whether the Russian elections should simply be canceled and if Yeltsin should remain as president for life. In *Izvestia* Mark Zakharov asks himself and others: "Are we really in such need of presidential elections in 1996?" He answers his own rhetorical question in the title of the article, "We Do Not Need Fateful Elections." But since any elections in Russia are now fateful, Zakharov could have used a shorter title: "We Do Not Need Elections." Russian democracy has thus managed to reject itself. Sometimes one feels like suggesting to today's democrats, "Shouldn't we perhaps restore the monarchy in Russia?" And serfdom along with it, to prevent the people from foolishly electing the Communists.

When I speak of Mark Zakharov I could cry. Why is such a marvelous director disgracing his name like that? He has not just now begun fawning on the authorities out of fear of a Communist restoration. A while ago I read his 1992 *Izvestia* article on his meeting with Yeltsin. He speaks of the head of state in the same reverential tone that people formerly used in writing about Lenin or Stalin. "He's simple, very simple, yet enigmatic." The writer Anatoli Pristavkin echoes Mark Zakharov. He has access to the president because he heads the presidential commission on pardons. When he was asked whether Yeltsin has changed recently, Pristavkin replied with a respectful sigh:

> Sometimes I remember what he looked like on the balcony of the White House [in August 1991]. A young face, such nice eyes—someone I was drawn to. Then I watched him at receptions and banquets. I think the rumors that he drinks a lot are unfounded. (Maybe a shot or two.) Some physical changes, though, may be reflected in his health. I think it's probably a result of his very heavy workload.

The sociologist Yulia Vishnevskaya rightly noted in *Sintaksis* that the similarity between the loyal ecstasy of the Russian intelligentsia at the beginning of the 1990s and people's behavior in the 1930s is quite striking. (Incidentally, a great deal of the material about the intelligentsia in this lecture came from a file of Vishnevskaya's with the telling title "Brownnoser.") But the more one thinks about these parallels in our recent history, the more striking the differences between that generation and ours. These differences are by no means in our favor. While our fathers and grandfathers had reasons for being misled regarding the true nature of the new Stalinist regime, such an attack of collective insanity is totally unforgivable in our contemporaries.

First, in our day there has been no period of terror in which the "brain of the nation" suddenly, inexplicably, and forever lost its mind. Second, the people who were born in the twenties and thirties are somewhat excused because they did not have the experience of those who had lived those decades. In our day, however, people adore the secretary of the Sverdlovsk *obkom* [Yeltsin] "as their own Stalin," and these are people such as Marietta Chudakova and Kronid Liubarsky,[13] who had devoted their entire lives to studying the experience of those generations and the consequences. Third, and most important, I believe the intellectuals of the earlier era could still have been misled regarding contemporary Leninist-Stalinist power, the power of the pioneers who had come to "fulfill the age-old dream of mankind," to do something totally unprecedented in world history.

What are the present Russian authorities offering the people? "Support Yeltsin and you'll live the way people do in America!" It is your duty as an intellectual to understand the world around you and to know that America is not an "age-old dream" but a very real country that has been very well studied. How is it possible not to see that everything in Russia is being done not "like in America" (or in France or Sweden), but the way things were done in Uganda under President Idi Amin?

Another striking characteristic of the "intelligentsia in the retinue of the president of Russia" should be noted. All the innumerable campaigns of the intelligentsia in support of Yeltsin included no representatives of the hard sciences; mostly actors and literary people were involved. This is particularly striking given the enormous role played by physicists and mathematicians in the human rights movement from the sixties to the eighties and later in the era of the Gorbachev transformations.

The intelligentsia overdid its toadying to Lenin, Stalin, Brezhnev, and finally to Yeltsin. Though today Yeltsin's stock is falling, and fewer say they love him, people are still banking on him. This is sometimes expressed in very strange ways. Look how the well-known journalist Oleg Moroz campaigns for the president in *Literaturnaya gazeta*:

> I'm gritting my teeth. I'm fighting nausea, but, as the lesser evil, he must be supported.

> Yeltsin unleashed the war in Chechnya and does not know how to extricate himself from it, and the Yeltsin regime has had many obvious failures. Property was given primarily to the bosses and the mafia, not to the people or to intelligent private owners.

> Under Yeltsin the bureaucracy grew enormously, and it knows no bounds. The scale of corruption and theft is fantastic. Criminals have become even more brazen. The police have gone off to get what they can from the stores and banks, and those who remained are fighting in Chechnya. Apparently there's no one else left to fight. The Yeltsin regime showed itself utterly incapable of regulating citizens' income, of keeping a ceiling on the earnings of the most

affluent, or of raising incomes for the most disadvantaged. Even more shocking is the fact that for many months he allowed a situation in which workers throughout the country were not paid their salaries.

The greatest blame for everything that has happened must be borne by Yeltsin himself. He is clearly incapable of daily, consistent, and focused work. He simply cannot manage to complete a single one of the projects he conceived or to control the implementation of his own decisions. Nevertheless, is there any need to demonstrate that no matter how weak Yeltsin may be as the country's leader, his replacement by a Communist president would be a thousand times more devastating for the nation? It would be a catastrophe, the road to the abyss. The country can no longer stand a Communist experiment, either materially or spiritually.

Literaturnaya gazeta, January 31, 1996

Not much of a choice. After all, Stalin originally was also theoretically (naturally, only theoretically) chosen by comparison to Trotsky. He was selected as the lesser evil, and subsequently turned out to be worse than the devil.

Another unequivocal democrat, the former dissident and camp inmate Lev Timofeev, has his own notions of democracy. He is proposing Aleksandr Solzhenitsyn, who is outside and above the parties, as president. Or, at worst, Timofeev would leave President Yeltsin in power. The Russian constitution, however, does not allow Aleksandr Isaevich to run for this high office because he lived abroad for too long. Should we perhaps abolish the constitution?

Thank God, everything is not yet lost, and there are still some democrats—democrats not set off in quotation marks. A commentator for the newspaper *Obshchaya gazeta*, Igor Shevelev, objects to Timofeev:

> The nomination of Aleksandr Isaevich as the country's leader looks odd, for it reflects a search for values and authorities that disappeared a long time ago. Perhaps the lack of truly popular individuals to play the role of the "father of the nation" is really the most valuable thing we have today. Perhaps we should simply select somebody for this government job and forget about it for a couple of years. The most important thing is that no individual interfere with our lives. Perhaps we will elect a president not to perform miracles and ensure progress and a radiant future, but to stop us from slitting each other's throats? When we get tired of that, the president, too, can become a normal individual. We'll forget who he is, a Communist, democrat, capitalist, or anyone else. Just a normal individual without any higher values. The church can perfectly well take care of these higher values.
>
> *Novaya gazeta*, January 12, 1996

This position comes very close to mine. When pondering the question of the president, however, democracy in Russia keeps looking for somebody who would be all things to all men, as if we were choosing a czar once and for all. We do not have a normal concept of power. We do not understand that power is not a czar, not God, and not the "father of the nation," that power is replaceable—periodically and regularly replaceable. Why does the intelligentsia continue to clutch at Yeltsin even though it does not expect anything particularly good from him? The only positive gain, the only value is the freedom of speech given to us by Gorbachev, which Yeltsin has not yet taken away. I have heard many times from all kinds of people: "As long as we can still write anything we want, we'll back Yeltsin." In 1992 the journalist Lev Sigal was ready for anything for the sake of this freedom to write:

> If the author of these lines could go back to 1985 and were once again faced with that choice: "You'll get freedom to speak, read, and write everything you want, but also poverty, national humiliation (national means the Soviet people), the splitting of the state and the emergence of 'flash points' within its former borders." Are you ready to follow such a twist of history and not say to yourself, "Well, you got what you wanted"? I would pause, sigh deeply, and say through my teeth, yes, let everything that is destined come to pass.

During the last few years this freedom of speech in Russia has undergone an incredible devaluation. A devaluation of words has taken place, which for an intellectual is more frightening than the devaluation of the ruble. The devaluation of speech took place in

75

two ways simultaneously: its price fell both in the eyes of the authorities and in the eyes of the intelligentsia. The Russian government, which in the past had had such a serious and painfully sensitive attitude to words that it imprisoned people for them, suddenly realized it was possible simply to spit on everything written in newspapers, magazines, and books. It acted in accordance with Grandfather Krylov's well-known fable "The Cat and the Cook." No matter how the loquacious cook (the independent press) abuses the miserable cat Vaska (power), who stole a chicken from the kitchen, "Vaska listens to him and keeps on eating."[14]

The government, incidentally, is already starting to show some claws:

> Yesterday upon his arrival in the Krasnodar region Vitali Ignatenko, the vice premier in charge of the mass media, explained to the local newspaper correspondents, printers, radio, and television journalists that "despite all its independence the Russian mass media must first and foremost express the state interests of Russia and comply with those interests."
>
> *Segodnya*, March 2, 1996

A similar thing happened to my Russian intelligentsia. As soon as the obstacles posed by the censorship disappeared, it stopped (or almost stopped) reading the press. Now, when I read a Russian newspaper "at home in France," be it an opposition or a progovernment paper, I never know whether my friends in Moscow have read it. And if they have, do they believe it? Quite recently we tried to tell Larisa Bogoraz, a former political exile and well-known human rights champion, a woman who could be called the grandmother of the dissident movement, about the teachers' hunger strikes and their disastrous situation (this information came from *Uchitelskaya gazeta*). This longtime fighter for freedom of speech said, "That's impossible! The papers write anything and everything!" That "anything and everything" expressed such contempt for freedom of speech that inevitably the question came to mind: "Was it worth making so many sacrifices for it? Perhaps we should close down all the newspapers and go back to samizdat? Remember how the intelligentsia literally tore the *Chronicle of Current Events* from each other's hands?" An anecdote from the Brezhnev era about a lady asking a typist to type out *War and Peace* comes to mind. "Why?" asks the astonished typist. "That's terribly expensive! Besides, it's sold in any bookstore." "You see," says the client, "my son doesn't read anything except samizdat, and I'd like him to read Tolstoy."

Despite glasnost and freedom of speech, Russia to a significant extent continues to remain a closed world. No one fully understands what decisions are taken at the very top and why they are taken, or how the country is being governed and by whom. Gleb Pavlovsky, a very talented journalist, came up with a striking definition of Yeltsin. Pavlovsky asserts that Yeltsin is a "collective pseudonym" and that it remains unclear who is governing Yeltsin. We could assume that, as a typical *obkom* secretary, Yeltsin is not capable of independent decisions. The job requires that he yield to whoever is stronger and that he oppress those who are weaker.

Yet these are only assumptions prompted by the generally confused picture of Russian life. Major political murders are taking place in the country along with murders in the field of business. All these murders remain unsolved. Who is behind the killings— and why—are questions shrouded in darkness.

Everyone knows that the bureaucracy is permeated by corruption, but no serious legal steps have been taken. The KGB has once again changed the sign on the wall and now has a different name. No one knows how far its power and influence extend and what it is in fact doing these days.

During the last few years my wife and I have spent a good deal of time in the Lubyanka Prison archives reading through the files of my case. I was not, however, allowed to see the files on how the case was prepared, who was following me, or who denounced me. Those files are all closed. I looked at the faces of the KGB people, and they were the same brazen old mugs. After 1991 they were quite polite and deferential. It's rather frightening to be sitting there next to the children and grandchildren of people who were killed during the purges. You see an old man who can't stand it any more and starts screaming, "I didn't sign that! I didn't sign that!" He's reading his interrogation from the thirties.

I was surprised by a question from a middle-aged woman who was interested in her father's case. She said: "Have you heard that perhaps not all the people who were sentenced to be shot were actually executed? Some of them were sent to the uranium mines." "Yes," I said, "I know that. Some of them were exiled." "Did you meet someone like that who was my father?" she asked.

Of course I never met him, and I'm sure he either died in the mines or was shot. Even though the KGB hasn't really fully opened up its shop, you get a rather terrible picture.

Against this muddy background the most gloomy refrains and fantastic hypotheses emerge, including the hoary argument of the Russian nationalist patriots that America is to blame for everything, since it is to America's advantage to have Russia weak and to transform a great power into a semicolonial market for Western junk.

In conclusion, I want to frighten you. Researchers are fond of comparing the territorial, demographic, geological, military, and cultural potential of various countries. The concept of organizational potential has appeared, and here the United States is traditionally in first place. One very important element, which I think everyone has forgotten, is missing from this range of potentials. That is the criminal potential, which is different for different peoples.

Thirty years ago at my trial the judge and the prosecutor kept hammering away at one phrase: "Russia is a country of thieves and drunks." At the time I was thinking of the Russian people's potential for theft, which Gorbachev failed to take into account when he began perestroika. That potential was significant, and it is extremely dangerous to forget about it. Speaking of the goals of perestroika, "to shake up society, wake it up, extricate it from its social apathy and indifference," Gorbachev said he intended to give "society the possibility to control the power of the people whom it elects."

But power is being controlled and administered not by society but by the criminal world, historically the most enterprising part of Russia. Why the most enterprising? Because in highly centralized and normative Soviet society, where any personal initiative was totally excluded, flashes of independent thinking were produced or preserved only by criminals—both political, that is, dissidents, and purely criminal individuals—facing the authorities. Sadly, the ideas and programs of criminals have proved to be stronger than those of the dissidents. It is therefore most regrettable that the problem of Russia and Democracy is of greater interest to sociologists and politicians than the problem of Russia and Crime.

The great Russian writer Aleksandr Solzhenitsyn used to frighten mankind with Communism. "Soon we will see everything without television screens," he stated, explaining that "the Third World War has already been lost," and that tomorrow or the day after tomorrow the Communist Soviet Union would seize the entire world. Everyone was very frightened. America spent colossal sums to support the struggle of various daredevils against totalitarian regimes. Other countries did not lag behind. Various demonstrations, committees, and international resistance movements did honor to mankind.

Once the Communists started calling themselves democrats, however, the world immediately stopped being afraid of us. Today I hear the Russian language everywhere. The Russian intelligentsia are not the only Russians strolling through Western museums and bookstores, or giving lectures at the Sorbonne or

Columbia University. The new contingent of Russians has British Home Secretary Michael Howard wringing his hands in despair: "Let us," he declares, "do everything in our power to put an end to the 'visa racket' that has allowed criminal elements from the former USSR to flood the United Kingdom." They launder enormous sums through the banks and companies of all the Western countries, sell Russian arms, and brazenly trade in drugs (*Literaturnaya gazeta*, January 31, 1996).

A virtually unimpeded seizure of foreign territory has begun. What kind of territory? One of the most striking examples is the occupation of the American radio station, Radio Liberty. You will recall how Soviet power fought with it for several decades, how it was unmasked in all the Soviet newspapers, how many times it was infiltrated by Soviet agents who poisoned and destroyed it, and how the security department of Radio Liberty examined each staff member inside out to check whether he didn't smack of communism.

And today? Without pain, without blood, without resistance, the American radio station has virtually ended up in Russian hands, and 90 percent of the time it plays up to the Russian czar. Similar things are happening in England with the BBC.

In analyzing what has taken place, I want to speak in the native language of my alter ego, the Odessa bandit Abram Tertz: "We shall not calm down. We shall overrun all your rich lands like locusts. We shall overrun them and devour them. We will not put up with foreign gold and foreign blood. We shall take over your banks, your palaces, your Côtes d'Azur, and your San Franciscos.

We are many and we are stronger. 'Yes, we are Scythians,' " as the unforgettable Abram Tertz said. " 'Yes, we are Asians, with slanting and greedy eyes!' "[15]

Abram Tertz differs from Andrei Sinyavsky. He's my literary mask and the mask of my literary style. He dots the i's. He spells things out. Sometimes his statements are a bit harsh. He says, "Yes, the Scythians are coming, they'll conquer you." That's why I gave him the floor at the very end. I said that I would be scaring you. It's not Sinyavsky who is frightening you. I gave the floor to him, my bandit double. Sinyavsky's view does not objectively exclude a serious danger, but this is not the danger presented by bandits or thieves who make their way to the West. It's hard now to emigrate from Russia and very difficult to get citizenship in another country. It's become a problem. Why? The West is putting up barriers and shielding itself against the Scythians. And the West is right to do that, although this is crippling many individual human fates and destinies.

NOTES

I, THE INTELLIGENTSIA AND THE PEOPLE

1. This is a paraphrase of Aleksandr Pushkin's poem "Druz'iam" (To friends) (1818):

   No, I am not a flatterer when I write
   And freely praise the czar.

   A. S. Pushkin, *Polnoe sobranie sochinenii v odnom tome* (Moscow: Gosudarstvennoe izdatel'stvo khudozhestvennoi literatury, 1949), 183.

2. The messianic concept of Russia as a "God-bearing" people with a divine mission to the world was developed by the Slavophiles and Dostoevsky. See Nicholas Berdyaev, *Dostoevsky* (Cleveland and New York: Meridian, 1964), 160.

3. "Every cook must be able to run the state" is a well-known saying of Lenin's.

4. This is a quote from the poem "Khorosho" (Good) (1927) by Vladimir Mayakovsky (1893–1930), an outstanding Futurist and lyric poet who praised the Revolution and the new regime in his very popular verses. Vladimir Mayakovsky, *Polnoe sobranie sochinenii v 13-i tomakh* (Moscow: Gosudarstvennoe izdatel'stvo khudozhestvennoi literatury, 1955–61), vol. 8, 324.

5. The economist Yegor Gaidar introduced "shock therapy" economic reforms in early 1992 by decontrolling consumer prices and ending state subsidies. Dismissed in December 1992, he became acting prime minister in 1993 and was excluded from the new government formed by Chernomyrdin in January 1994. He founded the political party The People's Choice.

6. Lazar Kaganovich (1893–1991) was a Politburo member under Stalin who played an important role in the purges of 1936–38. Kliment Voroshilov (1881–1969) served as defense minister and chairman of the presidium of the Supreme Soviet. Andrei Andreev was a member of the Politburo from 1932 to 1952 and a member of the presidium of the Supreme Soviet from 1953 to 1962. Andrei Zhdanov (1896–1948) was a central committee secretary and Leningrad party boss who tightened party control over writers and intellectuals during the post–World War II period.

7. Yuri Olesha (1899–1960), a novelist and playwright, author of *Zavist'* (Envy) (1927), was severely criticized by party authorities in the 1930s. Andrei Platonov (1899–1951) was an imaginative novelist and short story writer whose works were denounced and suppressed under Stalin. Mikhail Zoshchenko (1895–1958) was the author of popular satirical stories and sketches that were banned in the 1946 literary purge organized by Zhdanov. Paolo Iashvili (1895–1937) was a Georgian avant-garde symbolist poet and one of the organizers of the Georgian group of poets known as the Blue Horns. Isaac Babel (1894–1941), the Jewish author of the short story collections *Konarmiia* (Red cavalry) and *Odesskie rasskazy* (Odessa tales), was arrested in 1939 and perished in a labor camp. Yuri Tynianov (1884–1943) was a well-known formalist literary critic and the author of several historical novels.

8. Konstantin Paustovsky (1892–1968) was a novelist and short story writer known for his autobiography *Povest' o zhizni* (The story of my life). Pavel Antokol'sky (1896–1978) was a poet and translator; his collections of verse include *Vremia* (Time).

9. Vladimir Lugovskoi (1901–1957) was a poet whose collection *Pustynia i vesna* (The desert and spring) was written between 1930 and 1954.

10. Samuil Marshak (1887–1964) was a poet and translator whose poems for children and translations of Burns,

Wordsworth, Blake, and Kipling have become Russian literary classics.

11. Nikolai Tikhonov (1896–1979) wrote civic and lyric poetry. A political activist, he was the head of the Union of Soviet Writers (1944–1946) and from 1946 was a deputy of the Supreme Soviet.

12. Viktor Shklovsky (1893–1984), one of the founders of the formalist school, was a writer and literary critic.

13. Vsevolod Ivanov (1895–1963) was a prose writer of the ornamentalist school. His works on the civil war, *Bronepoezd No. 14–69* (Armored train no. 14–69) and *Tsvetnye vetra* (Colored winds), were widely read. Attacked by Soviet critics for "pessimism," he conformed to the system and became part of the establishment.

14. Sergei Averintsev is a philologist, member of the Duma, and chairman of the Russian Bible Society. Bella Akhmadulina is a popular lyric poet. The poet and songwriter Bulat Okudzhava is famous for the underground ballads he wrote and performed during the 1960s. Marietta Chudakova is a historian of twentieth-century Russian literature and an expert on the works of Mikhail Bulgakov.

15. Gennadi Zyuganov, leader of the Communist party of the Russian Federation, lost the 1996 presidential election to Boris Yeltsin. His party holds 30 percent of the seats in the Duma. Viktor Anpilov, longtime head of the Workers' Russia party, is a reactionary who has supported Zyuganov.

16. An eminent literary scholar and expert on Russian medieval literature, Academician Dmitri Likhachev has long been an active supporter of liberal causes in Russia. In 1990 he delivered the Harriman Lecture at Columbia University.

17. This is a line from the poem "Elegiia" (Elegy) (1874) by Nikolai Nekrasov (1821–1877). Nikolai Nekrasov, *Polnoe sobranie stikhotvorenii v trekh tomakh* (Leningrad: Sovetskii pisatel', 1967), vol. 2, 419–20.

18. Boris Zolotukhin is a Duma member and vice chairman of the Russia's Choice party.

19. This is from a speech by Chatsky, the hero of Aleksandr Griboyedov's play *Gore ot uma* (Woe from wit) (1822–1825), act 2, scene 2. A. S. Griboyedov, *Sochineniia v stikhakh* (Leningrad: Sovetskii pisatel', 1967), 90.

20. Nikolai Berdyaev (1874–1948) was a religious thinker and theologian who emigrated in 1922. His book *Russkaia ideia* (The Russian idea) is a classic of modern Russian thought.

21. Vassily Aksyonov is a writer and novelist who emigrated to the United States in 1980. His novels include *A Ticket to the Stars*, *The Burn*, and *In Search of Melancholy Baby*.

22. Konstantin Bal'mont (1867–1943) was an early symbolist poet and translator. After the Revolution he emigrated to France. The lines are from his poem "Revoliutsioner ia ili net" (Am I a revolutionary or not) (1918), in *Revoliutsioner ia ili net: Sbornik stikhotvorenii i statei* (Moscow: Verf', 1918), 39.

23. Aleksandr Blok (1880–1921) is Russia's most famous Symbolist poet. The lines are from his "Da. Tak diktuet vdokhnovenie" (Yes. So inspiration dictates), in *Sobranie sochinenii v 8-mi tomakh* (Moscow: Gosudarstvennoe izdatel'stvo khudozhestvennoi literatury, 1960), vol. 3, 93.

24. Sergei Kovalev is a long-standing campaigner for human rights who resigned as human rights adviser to Yeltsin in protest against the war in Chechnya.

25. Aleksandr Rutskoi, who became vice president in 1991, defied Yeltsin's order to disband the Parliament, and was arrested and imprisoned following the storming of the White House in October 1993. He was released under an amnesty in February 1994 and elected governor of the Kursk region in October 1996.

   Rustan Khasbulatov, a Chechen, was the speaker of the Supreme Soviet and a close confidant of Yeltsin who turned against him and lost power in October 1993.

2. THE INTELLIGENTSIA AND BREAD

1. The New Economic Policy (1921–28) was a temporary return to limited aspects of capitalism for all but large industrial enterprises. Stalin reversed NEP and replaced it with the First Five-Year Plan.

2. Piotr Stolypin (1862–1911), premier and minister of the interior for Nicholas II, at first attempted major social

reforms, especially land reform, but then moved to repress the revolutionary movement. He was assassinated in 1911.

3. Zoya Krakhmal'nikova is a Russian Orthodox writer who was jailed in the 1980s for her writings. Yevgeni Pasternak is the son of the writer Boris Pasternak.

4. Grigori Yavlinsky is a liberal economist and reformer, head of the Yabloko party. He was an unsuccessful candidate for president in the 1996 elections. His attempt to reform the Soviet economy in 1990 encountered strong opposition and failed.

5. The reference is to a poem by the peasant poet Sergei Esenin (1895–1925), "Shagane ty moia, Shagane" (Shagane, my Shagane), in *Sobranie sochinenii v shesti tomakh* (Moscow: Khudozhestvennaia literatura, 1977), vol. 1, 277.

6. Stanislav Govorukhin is a popular film director who won election to the Duma from St. Petersburg in 1993 and 1996. His films include *The Hour of the Scoundrel*.

7. Milovan Djilas's book *The New Class* (1957) was a scathing critique of the new class of top Communist bureaucrats and leaders in Yugoslavia whose abuse of power and privilege contradicted the principles of Communist egalitarian ideology.

8. Anders Aslund and Jeffrey Sachs are American economists who, as advisers to the Russian government in the early 1990s, promoted "shock therapy" to implement market reforms.

3. THE INTELLIGENTSIA AND DEMOCRACY

1. The line is from Pushkin's novel in verse *Evgenii Onegin*, chapter 8, stanza 2. Pushkin, *Polnoe sobranie sochinenii v odnom tome*, 500. The reference is to the elderly poet Gavrila Derzhavin (1743–1816) going down into his grave and giving his blessing to Pushkin and the young generation of poets.

2. A humorous conceit: the Marquis Astolphe de Custine in 1839 wrote an account of his trip to Russia in which he criticized the country as a hopeless bureaucratic autocracy. See his *Lettres de Russie: La Russie en 1839* (Paris: Gallimard, 1975).

3. Pavel Miliukov (1859–1943) was a leader of the Cadet (Constitutional Democratic) party in the short-lived Duma of 1906. Alexander Kerensky (1881–1970) headed the provisional government following the February revolution of 1917.

4. Aleksandr Nevzorov is a nationalistic television investigative journalist, commentator, and Duma deputy ("600 Seconds" is among his best-known programs).

5. These are words from Isaak Dunaevsky's popular "Pesnia o rodine" (Song about the Motherland), written in the early 1930s.

6. Along with Georgi Malenkov and Vyacheslav Molotov, Nikolai Bulganin made up the troika that governed the Soviet Union after Stalin's death in 1953.

7. Vyacheslav Kostikov was Yeltsin's press secretary until 1994, when he was appointed Russian ambassador to the Vatican. His memoirs, published in February 1996, were critical of Yeltsin.

8. Galina Starovoitova was elected to the Duma in 1996 as an independent candidate for St. Petersburg.

9. The reference is to Ivan Krylov's (1769–1844) fable of the wolf and the dogs, in which the wolf is chosen czar. Ivan Krylov, "Volk na psarne," *Polnoe sobranie sochinenii* (Moscow: Gosudarstvennoe izdatel'stvo khudozhestvennoi literatury, 1945–46), vol. 3, 66.

10. Georgi Fedotov (1886–1951) was a Russian Orthodox religious thinker and historian.

11. Iosif Kobzon is a wealthy popular singer who in March 1996 won a libel case against the newspaper *Sovetskaya rossiya*, which had charged that he was connected with organized crime. He was denied a United States visa in 1995 as a result of similar reports in the *Washington Post*.

12. Andrei Bitov is a novelist, president of the Russian chapter of PEN, and author of the trilogy *The Monkey Link*.

13. Kronid Liubarsky is a journalist, veteran human rights activist, and deputy editor of *Novoe vremia*.

14. The reference is to Ivan Krylov's fable "Kot i povar" (The cat and the cook). Krylov, *Polnoe sobranie sochinenii* (Moscow: Gosudarstvennoe izdatel'stvo khudozhestvennoi literatury, 1945–46), vol. 3, 65.

15. The lines are from Aleksandr Blok's poem "Skify" (The

Scythians) (1918), in which the Scythians (the Russians) warn the outside world of Russia's primeval strength, given a new impetus by the Revolution. Aleksandr Blok, *Sobranie sochinenii v 8-mi tomakh* (Moscow: Gosudarstvennoe izdatel'stvo khudozhestvennoi literatury, 1960), vol. 3, 360.

INDEX